W9-BMT-661

The Black Press

Lucent Library of Black History

Carla Mooney

LUCENT BOOKS
A part of Gale, Cengage Learning

Detroit • New York • San Francisco • New Haven, Conn • Waterville, Maine • London

LIBRARY OF CONGRESS CATALOGING-IN-PUBLICATION DATA

Mooney, Carla, 1970–
The Black press / by Carla Mooney.
p. cm. -- (Lucent library of Black history)
Includes bibliographical references and index.
ISBN 978-1-4205-0230-5 (hardcover)
1. African American press--History--19th century. 2. African American press--History--20th century. I. Title.
PN4882.5M58 2010
071'.308996073--dc22

2009040774

Lucent Books
27500 Drake Rd.
Farmington Hills, MI 48331

ISBN-13: 978-1-4205-0230-5
ISBN-10: 1-4205-0230-1

Printed in the United States of America
1 2 3 4 5 6 7 14 13 12 11 10

Printed by Bang Printing, Brainerd, MN, 1st Ptg., 03/2010

Contents

Foreword

It has been more than 500 years since Africans were first brought to the New World in shackles, and over 140 years since slavery was formally abolished in the United States. Over 50 years have passed since the fallacy of "separate but equal" was obliterated in the American courts, and some 40 years since the watershed Civil Rights Act of 1965 guaranteed the rights and liberties of all Americans, especially those of color. Over time, these changes have become celebrated landmarks in American history. In the twenty-first century, African American men and women are politicians, judges, diplomats, professors, deans, doctors, artists, athletes, business owners, and home owners. For many, the scars of the past have melted away in the opportunities that have been found in contemporary society. Observers such as Peter N. Kirsanow, who sits on the U.S. Commission of Civil Rights, point to these accomplishments and conclude, "The growing black middle class may be viewed as proof that most of the civil rights battles have been won."

In spite of these legal victories, however, prejudice and inequality have persisted in American society. In 2003, African Americans comprised just 12 percent of the nation's population, yet accounted for 44 percent of its prison inmates and 24 percent of its poor. Racially motivated hate crimes continue to appear on the pages of major newspapers in many American cities. Furthermore, many African Americans still experience either overt or muted racism in their daily lives. A 1996 study undertaken by Professor Nancy Krieger of the Harvard School of Public Health, for example, found that 80 percent of the African American participants reported having experienced racial discrimination in one or more settings, including at work or school, applying for housing and medical care, from the police or in the courts, and on the street or in a public setting.

It is for these reasons that many believe the struggle for racial equality and justice is far from over. These episodes of discrimination threaten to shatter the illusion that America has completely overcome its racist past, causing many black Americans to become increasingly frustrated and confused. Scholar and writer Ellis Cose has described this splintered state in the following way: "I have done everything I was supposed to do. I have stayed out of trouble with the law, gone to the right schools, and worked myself nearly to death. What more do they want? Why in God's name won't they accept me as a full human being?" For Cose and others, the struggle for equality and justice has yet to be fully achieved.

In many subtle yet important ways the traumatic experiences of slavery and segregation continue to inform the way race is discussed and experienced in the twenty-first century. Indeed, it is possible that America will always grapple with the fallout from its distressing past. Ulric Haynes, dean of the Hofstra University School of Business has said, "Perhaps race will always matter, given the historical circumstances under which we came to this country." But studying this past and understanding how it contributes to present-day dialogues about race and history in America is a critical component of contemporary education. To this end, the Lucent Library of Black History offers a thorough look at the experiences that have shaped the black community and the American people as a whole. Annotated bibliographies provide readers with ideas for further research, while fully documented primary and secondary source quotations enhance the text. Each book in the series explores a different episode of black history; together they provide students with a wealth of information as well as launching points for further study and discussion.

Introduction

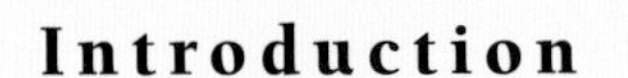

A Voice for the Black Community

"We wish to plead our own cause,"[1] wrote the founders of *Freedom's Journal*, the country's first black newspaper. These words rang true for the *Journal* and the hundreds of black newspapers that would follow. The black press gave a voice to black people in America when they had few options and resources. Said Vernon Jarrett, a journalist with the black press in the 1940s:

> We didn't exist in the early papers. We were never born, we didn't get married, we didn't die. We didn't fight in any wars. We never participated in anything of scientific achievement. We were truly invisible, unless we committed a crime. But in the black press, we did get married. They showed us our babies being born. They showed us graduating. They showed our Ph.D.'s.[2]

Since the first paper in 1827, the black press has been a force in American history. It became a key weapon in the black community's struggle for freedom and equal treatment. The black press fought for freedom of slaves during the antebellum period. After the Civil War black papers educated blacks and helped them form an identity. As violence and lynchings increased, black papers led the fight against the violence. They protested for equal treatment of black soldiers during two world wars. They also spoke out for equal treatment and civil rights for all Americans, regardless of race.

In history classes many have learned about legendary black figures like Martin Luther King Jr., Harriet Tubman, and Rosa Parks. The editors of black newspapers, however, are the lesser-known heroes in the black community's struggle for equality. Although they receive less attention, their efforts are no less important. Black journalists like Samuel Cornish, Robert Abbott, Ida B. Wells, and Robert Vann were instrumental in fighting for

The black press spoke out for equal treatment throughout history, especially during the civil rights movement.

civil rights. They were more than journalists; they were also leaders of the black community. These men and women stood up in the face of great odds to fight for the black community.

From the beginning the editor's job was not easy. The struggle for funding was constant. Every day these men and women worked to keep their papers in print. They sold subscriptions and searched for advertising dollars. Many papers survived for a few years on donations or the editor's personal money. Without enough money many black papers only lasted a few months or years.

Editors of black newspapers also had to be careful about what they printed in their papers. They had to be bold and strong but also smart. Readers wanted a strong voice to speak out against unfairness and unequal treatment. Yet speaking out too much, especially in the South, could jeopardize the paper. Whites often monitored what black papers wrote. When angered by a black newspaper, white mobs would destroy the offending newspaper's office. If the editor did not get out of sight quickly enough, he or she also risked being run out of town, physically harmed, or even killed.

Despite the risks and challenges, black newspapers effectively delivered their message. They loudly called for civil and social rights. They also provided a place for black Americans to debate current issues. Although the black papers' strongest role was as a protester, they also delivered black community news. Black papers printed local news and notices of births, deaths, and marriages. For the first time blacks had a place to read news written for them.

The black press reached the height of its power and influence in the 1940s and 1950s. The success of strong papers like the *Chicago Defender* and the *Pittsburgh Courier* fueled its rise during this time. Like the first black papers nearly a century earlier, these papers relentlessly protested injustice and unfair treatment in America.

The civil rights movement of the 1960s triggered the decline of the black press. During these years, the black press's competition increased. White newspapers and television news covered the civil rights movement as it happened. For the first time black readers had a choice on where to find news about their community. White papers also opened their doors to black journalists, hiring away some of the black press's best talent. As readers turned to other sources, many black papers went out of business.

The passage of civil rights legislation in the 1960s achieved many of the black press's long-standing goals. The importance of the black press in this achievement cannot be overstated. For almost two hundred years, the black press has been a symbol of hope, pride, and unity for black Americans. In the words of Dorothy Gilliam, a legendary black journalist with the *Washington Post*, "From antebellum days through the Reconstruction to the Civil Rights movement, the black press has had a unique and important role in helping some blacks become part of the mainstream and others to succeed against formidable odds."[3]

Chapter One

The Birth of the Black Press

In the winter of 1827, a group of black men gathered in New York City at the home of Boston Crummell, a former slave who had walked away from his master after announcing that he would no longer serve him. They were outraged by the latest writings of Mordecai Manuel Noah, the editor of the *New York Enquirer* newspaper. In an editorial titled "Piracy and Murder," Noah wrote: "The fifteenth part of the population of this city is composed of Blacks; only fifteen are qualified to vote. Freedom is a great blessing indeed to them. They swell our list of paupers, they are indolent and uncivil; and yet if a Black man commits a crime, we have more interest made for him than for a white."[4] Tired of Noah's constant insults in the *Enquirer*, the men decided it was time to respond. They chose one of the only weapons they had—the written word.

Not Truly Free

For free blacks living in New York and other northern cities in the 1820s, life was not easy. For a black person, simply walking down the street could be dangerous. White people harassed black men, women, and children. White mobs disrupted black businesses, churches, and community celebrations.

Only a few decades earlier, Americans had fought for freedom from England. The country's founders famously wrote about equal rights in the Declaration of Independence: "We hold these truths to be self-evident, that all men are created equal, that they are endowed by their Creator with certain unalienable Rights, that among them are Life, Liberty and the pursuit of Happiness."[5] For black Americans equal treatment was nearly impossible to find.

Blacks faced discrimination at work, school, and church. Most worked in low-paying, unskilled jobs. Blacks with the skills to be carpenters, tailors, and blacksmiths could only find low-paying positions as porters, barbers, waiters, cooks, and maids. As European immigrants arrived, they competed with free blacks for these jobs. Often employers hired the white Europeans and fired the black workers. In addition, most schools were highly restricted or closed to blacks. Churches and other places of worship were segregated.

Blacks also faced discrimination when trying to vote. In the early 1800s the New York legislature changed the law to make it harder for blacks to vote. Under the new law white men only had to be taxpayers in order to vote. Black men, however, had to meet stricter requirements. To vote, a black man had to be twenty-one

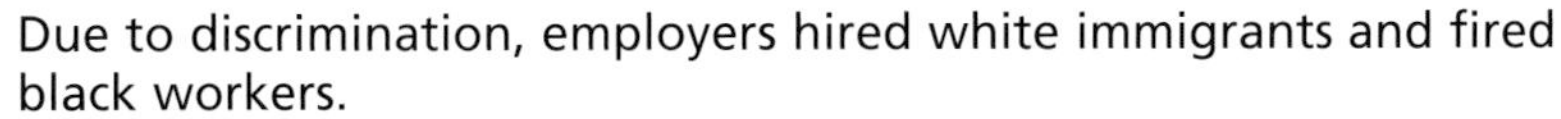

Due to discrimination, employers hired white immigrants and fired black workers.

years old, live for at least three years in New York, and own property worth at least $250.

Although free, blacks in the pre–Civil War northern states had few choices. They had limited access to jobs, education, and voting rights. As a result, they had little opportunity to build a successful life.

Spreading a Stereotype

To make matters worse, white Americans wrote and controlled the newspapers of the day. Many of them rarely reported on events of interest to black people. When they did they usually painted a picture of blacks as less human than whites. White papers said that black people were not educated. They claimed blacks had no morals and were criminals. The white press also printed posters and cartoons with the black man as an object of ridicule.

The *New York Enquirer* was one of the most influential papers of the time. Its founder and editor, Mordecai Manuel Noah, was a lawyer and playwright. He openly disliked black people. Time after time he used his position at the *Enquirer* to write insulting articles about black people. Noah also thought that free black people should be sent back to Africa.

The First Amendment to the Constitution granted the right of free speech and press. Under this amendment, white papers were free to print what they wished. Many times, however, that was a false and negative picture of black people.

Speaking Out for Black Rights

Black leaders and white abolitionists disagreed with the white community's treatment of black citizens. They believed that all people, regardless of color, should have the same rights and opportunities in the United States. They wanted everyone to be treated fairly. White abolitionists and black preachers spoke out for black rights in the North. They argued for freedom from slavery in the South. Still, spreading a message through speech was slow work. Speeches only touched the few people who attended and heard them. Newspapers, on the other hand, could reach many more people. People in opposite ends of the city could read a newspaper at the same time. Also, a message in print had a more lasting impact.

White abolitionists, like the Pennsylvania Abolition Society, were against the poor treatment of black citizens.

Some whites formed newspapers to speak out against slavery. Black activists subscribed to and supported these papers. Even though they were published with help from blacks, these papers were still white owned and controlled.

The First Black Press

The men meeting at Boston Crummell's house decided the best way to fight for black rights was through the pages of their own newspaper. They named their press *Freedom's Journal*. It would be the nation's first completely black newspaper. Black owners would hire black editors. They would write for the black people and feature issues and articles of interest to the black community.

The *Journal*'s first goal was to respond to the unflattering picture of blacks painted by Noah's *Enquirer* and other white newspapers. The *Journal*'s prospectus announced the new business:

American Colonization Society

Paul Cuffee was a successful black shipowner who supported free blacks returning to Africa. In 1816 Cuffee made one voyage, taking thirty-eight American blacks to Freetown, Sierra Leone. His death in 1817 ended any future trips.

Cuffee's arguments for colonization gathered attention. In 1817 the American Colonization Society formed with the mission of sending free blacks to Africa. The society helped establish a colony on the west coast of Africa called Liberia. By 1867 the society had assisted the move of thirteen thousand blacks to Liberia.

The idea of colonization divided blacks and whites. Some blacks supported the idea. They thought blacks could never achieve equal status in America. Others believed blacks should stay and fight for civil rights and slavery's end. Even whites who supported colonization had different reasons. Some saw the plan as a way to rid the country of blacks. Others felt blacks might be happier in Africa and could help civilize African natives.

Abolitionists attacked the society. They tried to discredit colonization. Still the society pressed on in its beliefs. By the Civil War's end, however, the society's support declined. The society eventually turned its efforts toward education and Liberian missions. It was eventually dissolved in 1964.

> We shall ever regard the constitution of the United States as our polar star. Pledged to no party, we shall endeavor to urge our brethren to use their right to the elective franchise [right to vote] as free citizens. . . . Daily slandered, we think that there ought to be some channel of communion between us and the public, through which a single voice may be heard, in defense of five hundred thousand free people of colour. For often [have] injustices been heaped up us, when our only defense was an appeal to the Almighty: but we believe that the time has now arrived, when the calumnies of our enemies should be refuted by forcible arguments.[6]

The founders of the *Journal* also believed a paper could unite black people across the country. They would use it to speak out about the major black issues of the time, slavery and civil rights.

The Editors

To lead *Freedom's Journal*, the founders chose two young men, John B. Russwurm and the Reverend Samuel E. Cornish. These men were among the most promising talents in New York.

Cornish was born in 1795 to free black parents in Delaware. In his early twenties, he left his family home to teach in a Philadelphia school for blacks. Cornish also became a minister. He organized the first black Presbyterian church in New York City. Like many black leaders Cornish worked to end slavery. He founded several antislavery associations and worked with abolition organizations. In

John Russwurm founded *Freedom's Journal* and was one of the first black men to graduate from an American college.

Philadelphia and New York, Cornish saw the struggles of the black community. He was convinced that living conditions needed to be improved. If that did not happen, Cornish believed blacks would never truly be a free people. Cornish understood the power of newspapers. He knew they had helped unite the colonies during the Revolutionary War. Now he saw newspapers as a way to fight hatred, slander, and the abuse of black people.

Russwurm was a freeborn black born in Jamaica in 1799. His father was a white planter from Virginia, and his mother was a black housekeeper. When Russwurm was eight years old, his father sent him to school in Canada. In 1826, he graduated from Bowdoin College in Maine, making him one of the first black men to graduate from an American college. After college Russwurm moved to New York City. There he became a well-spoken and dedicated leader in the antislavery movement.

Freedom's Journal helped give a voice to the black community.

The First Issue Debuts

After the meeting at Crummell's house, Cornish and Russwurm set to work. They set up operations at No. 5 Varick Street in Manhattan. Their offices were right in the middle of the city's printing and publishing industry. On March 16, 1827, the first issue of *Freedom's Journal* hit the streets. It was a four-page paper that measured 10 by 15 inches (25.4 by 38.1cm). Four columns of text ran vertically down each page. The editors chose a motto, "Righteousness Exalteth a Nation," from a verse in the Bible's book of Proverbs. They placed the motto on the front page directly beneath the name *Freedom's Journal*.

At first glance *Freedom's Journal* may not have seemed very different from other papers. A closer look, however, showed how different it really was. It was the only paper in which all news, articles, and ads were written for black readers.

"To Our Patrons"

Cornish and Russwurm did not know how their paper would be received by the public. On the front page of the first issue, they wrote a letter to their readers. It began, "In presenting our first [paper] to our patrons, we feel all the [uncertainty] in persons entering upon a new and untried line of business."[7]

The letter to readers took up almost three full columns on the front page of the *Journal*. It laid out the purpose of the *Journal* and what the editors hoped to accomplish. First and foremost it gave a voice to the black community.

> We wish to plead our own cause. Too long have others spoken for us. Too long has the publick been deceived by misrepresentations, in things which concern us dearly, though in the estimation of some mere trifles; for though there are many in society who exercise towards us benevolent feelings; still (with sorrow we confess it) there are others who make it their business to enlarge upon the least trifle, which tends to the discredit of any person of colour.[8]

In their front-page letter, the editors also wrote about the importance of learning. They strongly believed that education was the key to success in life. To help blacks they decided to use the paper as a tool to educate and inform readers. "Education being an object of

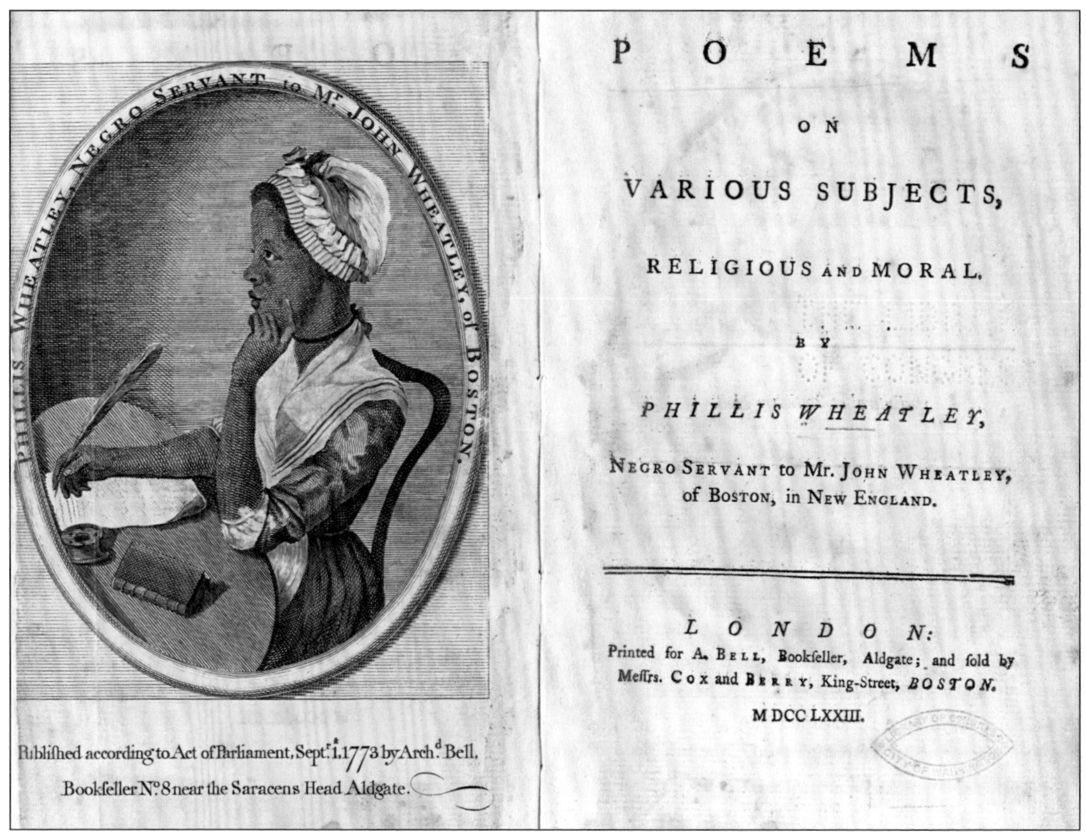
PHILLIS WHEATLEY, NEGRO SERVANT to Mr. JOHN WHEATLEY, of BOSTON.

Publiſhed according to Act of Parliament, Sept. 1. 1773 by Arch.d Bell, Bookſeller No. 8 near the Saracens Head Aldgate.

POEMS

ON

VARIOUS SUBJECTS,

RELIGIOUS AND MORAL.

BY

PHILLIS WHEATLEY,

NEGRO SERVANT to Mr. JOHN WHEATLEY, of BOSTON, in NEW ENGLAND.

LONDON:

Printed for A. BELL, Bookſeller, Aldgate; and ſold by Meſſrs. COX and BERRY, King-Street, *BOSTON*.

MDCCLXXIII.

Poet Phyllis Wheatley was a successful African American who inspired *Freedom's Journal* readers.

the highest importance to the welfare of society, we shall endeavour to present just and adequate views of it, and to urge upon our brethren the necessity and expediency of training their children . . . thus forming them for becoming useful members of society."[9]

The editors also asked its readers to support civil rights for all black people: "The civil rights of a people being of the greatest value, it shall ever be our duty to vindicate our brethren, when oppressed, and to lay the case before the publick."[10]

A New Edition Every Week

Cornish and Russwurm published a new copy of the *Journal* each week. Editorials spoke out against slavery and lynching. They also called for political rights and the right to vote. The *Journal* ran articles about life and news in foreign countries like Haiti and Sierra Leone, where free blacks lived, to expand the worldview of readers.

The *Journal* tried to set a good example for readers. The editors ran biographies of successful black figures, such as poet Phillis Wheatley, to inspire readers. Other articles gave advice about life, like how to select friends and face problems head-on.

The *Journal* became a paper of record for the black community. For the first time black people could read about events in their own

Walker's Appeal

David Walker was a writer for *Freedom's Journal* and a leader of Boston's antislavery movement. In September 1829 he published his own pamphlet titled *Walker's Appeal*. It became one of the most inflammatory antislavery documents of its time.

Walker called for his fellow countrymen to end slavery, even if it led to violence. He wrote:

> Let no man of us budge one step. . . . America is more our country, than it is the whites—we have enriched it with our blood and tears. The greatest riches in all America have arisen from our blood and tears:—and will they drive us from our property and homes, which we have earned with our blood? They must look sharp or this very thing will bring swift destruction upon them.[1]

Walker's Appeal sparked immediate controversy. His words inspired slaves but angered slaveholders. Southern whites offered a reward for Walker's head. Friends urged Walker to flee to safety in Canada, but he refused. "Somebody must die in this cause. I may be doomed to the stake and the fire, or to the scaffold tree, but it is not in me to falter if I can promote the work of emancipation,"[2] Walker said.

In 1830 Walker died at home. Although there was no evidence, some believed he was murdered. Others believe tuberculosis killed Walker.

1. David Walker, *Walker's Appeal*, Africans in America, PBS. www.pbs.org/wgbh/aia/part4/4h2931t.html.

2. Quoted in Africans in America, "People & Events: David Walker," PBS. www.pbs.org/wgbh/aia/part4/4p2930.html.

neighborhoods. The *Journal* ran birth and death notices and wedding announcements. It also featured ads for jobs and housing.

Spreading the Word

At its peak the *Journal* had forty-four agents to sell subscriptions. A yearlong subscription cost three dollars, half of which had to be paid up front. Agents sold the *Journal* in eleven states. They also sold the paper in the District of Columbia, Canada, Haiti, and England. Historians estimate the *Journal* sold about eight hundred copies per week. At the same time the largest white newspaper in New York sold about four thousand copies per week.

Free blacks and slaves as far south as Virginia and Maryland read the *Journal*. For slaves, however, reading was forbidden. Being caught with the *Journal* usually brought severe punishment.

Editorial Disagreements

Within a few months tensions between Cornish and Russwurm rose. The two men stood on opposite sides of an important issue of the time. In the early 1800s the idea of African colonization was debated. African colonization was an idea to send free blacks back to Africa. Some people, mostly whites, supported colonization. A group of supporters called the American Colonization Society helped to form a colony on the west coast of Africa called Liberia where blacks could move. Most blacks, however, had lived their whole lives in America and did not want to travel to a foreign land.

Russwurm supported colonization. He believed that the hatred many whites felt for blacks in the United States was too strong and deep to overcome. In his opinion colonization was the best way for blacks to get full freedom and civil rights.

Cornish, on the other hand, believed that blacks should stay and fight for their civil rights in America. After six months he decided he could no longer work with Russwurm. He resigned his role as editor of the paper. He did, however, continue to work for the *Journal* as a general agent.

Decline of the *Journal*

After Cornish resigned, Russwurm kept publishing weekly copies of the *Journal*. In the months that followed, his support of colonization grew. He wrote on March 14, 1829:

> We have said so much lately on the subject of colonization . . . the more anxious we are to throw light on the subject by holding up the present state of the colony at Liberia, and also by contrasting our present condition, with the far happier one of our Liberian brethren who are at present enjoying all the privileges and advantages to which their more active enterprise affords them.[11]

Readers did not like Russwurm's support of colonization. Blacks who had read the paper for the past two years now turned away from it. Money from sales, ads, and private investors dropped. Without an income stream, the paper could no longer support itself.

On March 28, 1829, Russwurm published the *Journal*'s final issue. In it he wrote one last letter about the difficulties of the job:

> Generally speaking an editor's office is a thankless one and if so among an enlightened people: what could we expect? We are therefore not in the least astonished, that we have been slandered by the villainous that our name is byword among the more ignorant, for what less could we expect. Prepared, we entered the lists; and unvanquished to retire, with the hope that the talent committed to our care, may yet be exerted under more favorable auspices, and upon minds more like to appreciate its value.[12]

Eight months later Russwurm left the United States for Africa. He settled in Liberia, where he started a newspaper called the *Liberia Herald*. He also became involved in the country's politics until his death in 1851.

Rights of All

After Russwurm resigned from the paper, the paper's owners were in a bind. They had a newspaper to publish but no editor at the helm. They asked Samuel Cornish to take the reins of the paper once again. This time the paper would run under a new name, *Rights of All*.

The first issue of *Rights of All* was printed on May 29, 1829. Cornish tried to make it an entirely new paper. He also made it clear that he did not agree with Russwurm's position on colonization. He

Samuel Cornish did not agree with Russwurm about colonization and started his own paper, *Rights of All.*

wrote, "The sudden change of the late Editor of the *Freedom's Journal* in respect to colonization excited much astonishment and led to many inquiries; to me the subject is equally strange as to others, and I can only dispose of it, by classing it with the other novelties of the day."[13]

Unfortunately, the damage done by Russwurm carried over to *Rights of All*. The new paper struggled to find a base of readers.

Five months later, on October 9, 1829, Cornish printed the paper's final issue.

Laying the Foundation

Freedom's Journal only lasted two years. Still it had a lasting impact on the black struggle for human and civil rights. For the first time a newspaper showed blacks as parents, workers, and social human beings. It challenged the racial stereotypes put forth by the white press. The *Journal* brought antislavery writings to blacks living as far south as Virginia and Maryland, and it created a sense of unity in the black community. It also encouraged hope. In two short years *Freedom's Journal* paved the way for black newspapers to come.

Chapter Two

Antebellum Papers and the Civil War

In the years before the Civil War, tensions between northern and southern states grew. Men fiercely debated whether slavery should be allowed in new states and territories. In 1850 Congress passed the Fugitive Slave Act, which required the federal government to assist in returning runaway slaves. When captured, blacks were not allowed to present evidence or testify about their free status. As a result, many northern blacks feared bounty hunters would capture and return them to slavery. Whites, on the other hand, feared slave revolts. Their fears increased when a Virginia slave named Nat Turner led the country's bloodiest slave rebellion in 1831. More than fifty whites were killed before authorities captured Turner and put him to death.

Increasing Discrimination

Turner's revolt led to increased discrimination against free blacks. It caused more northern and southern whites to speak publicly in favor of slavery. In 1832 respected professor Thomas R. Dew of William and Mary College wrote a defense of slavery:

> A merrier being does not exist on the face of the globe, than the negro slave of the United States . . . they are

> happy and contented, and the master much less cruel than is generally imagined. Why then, since the slave is happy, and happiness is the great object of all animated creation, should we endeavor to disturb his contentment by infusing into his mind a vain and indefinite desire for liberty—a something which he cannot comprehend, and which must inevitably dry up the very sources of his happiness.[14]

Dew's arguments strengthened the proslavery feelings of whites. His writings were also a key factor in stalling antislavery movements in the South.

Abolitionist Protest

As proslavery feelings rose, abolitionists stepped up their efforts against slavery in the northern states. One of these men, William Lloyd Garrison, was the publisher of the abolitionist newspaper the *Liberator*. In December 1832 he blasted: "People of New-England, and of the free States! Is it true that slavery is no concern of yours? Have you no right even to protest against it, or to seek its removal? . . . Awake to your danger! The struggle is a mighty one—it cannot be avoided—it should not be, if it could."[15] Many free blacks read Garrison's paper. Still they longed for a press of their own again.

William Lloyd Garrison published the *Liberator* for over thirty years.

The *Colored American*

A new black paper finally emerged in 1837. After *Rights of All* closed, editor Samuel Cornish remained active in the antislavery and black rights movements. He returned to journalism and became the editor of a new paper, the *Colored American*. The paper's proprietor, Philip A. Bell, had first called it the *Weekly Advocate*. Two months later the men changed the paper's name to the *Colored American*. They wanted the paper to be more easily recognized as a black press.

Some people criticized the new name. The men explained their choice in the paper's March 4, 1837, issue:

William Lloyd Garrison and the *Liberator*

After *Freedom's Journal* and *Rights of All* closed, the white abolitionist press stepped in to fill the void. William Lloyd Garrison was one of the most famous and radical abolitionists in the years before the Civil War. He called for immediate freedom for all slaves. His views were often unpopular, but Garrison believed that blacks and whites should be equal in every way in the United States.

On January 1, 1831, Garrison published the first issue of his abolitionist newspaper, the *Liberator*. He wrote: "I do not wish to think, or speak, or write, with moderation. . . . I am in earnest—I will not equivocate—I will not excuse—I will not retreat a single inch—AND I WILL BE HEARD."

In each weekly issue Garrison and the *Liberator* spoke out against slavery and the abuses suffered by the black community. Many of his subscribers were free blacks who had probably read *Freedom's Journal* or *Rights of All*. For three decades the paper sent its message to readers. When the Civil War ended slavery, Garrison felt the *Liberator*'s mission was completed. More than thirty years after the first issue, Garrison published the last issue of the *Liberator* on December 29, 1865.

Quoted in Africans in America, "People & Events: William Lloyd Garrison," PBS. www.pbs.org/wgbh/aia/part4/4p1561.html.

> Many would gladly rob us of the endeared name, "Americans," a distinction more emphatically belonging to us, than five-sixths of this nation and one that we will never yield. . . . But why colored? Some have said: why draw this cord of cast? how, then, shall we be known and our interests presented in community, but by some distinct, specific name—and what appellation is so inoffensive, so acceptable as COLORED PEOPLE—COLORED AMERICANS.[16]

The *Colored American*'s goal was to improve the lives of free blacks and achieve freedom for slaves. Published weekly, the paper usually ran between four and six pages. Each issue featured news about abolitionist activity and black rights issues.

In editorials the *Colored American* responded to white proslavery arguments. One editorial printed on July 8, 1837, said:

> How long will Americans,—the sons of the Pilgrims, turn a deaf ear to the cries of oppressed humanity, and to the warning voice of God?—How long will they keep up these invidious distinctions? Shall the creatures of God . . . indulge in prejudices against their brethren, made in the same image of God, merely because they differ from themselves in complexion?[17]

Like many black papers before the Civil War, the *Colored American* had financial problems. It relied on money from subscribers and donations to survive. Despite several fund-raising drives, money was always tight. Sometimes several weeks would pass between issues. The money problems eventually caused Cornish to resign after twenty-seven months as editor. He felt he could not support his family with the money he earned at the paper. The paper continued after Cornish left, until its final issue on December 25, 1841.

Black Journalism Emerges

Even though early papers had closed, the seeds of journalism had been planted. Before the Civil War more than forty black newspapers emerged. Most were small and short-lived. All protested the lack of civil rights for northern free blacks and southern slaves. The papers' names, like the *Freeman's Advocate*, *Genius of*

First Black Magazines

The first black magazine, the *Mirror of Liberty*, was published off and on in New York City between 1837 and 1840. David Ruggles published and edited the monthly *Mirror*. Ruggles helped organize the New York Committee of Vigilance, which assisted fugitive slaves. The *Mirror* became the group's official press. It called for laws to protect free citizens from being kidnapped and returned into slavery. It also supported laws to ensure the right of trial by jury. Unfortunately, the magazine was shortlived. Ruggles's poor health forced the *Mirror* to cease publication in 1840.

A second black magazine, the *National Reformer*, appeared in Philadelphia in 1838. It was the official press of founder William Whipper's American Moral Reform Society. The *National Reformer* featured articles on self-improvement, self-help, and racial unity. It also called for full citizen rights for all blacks. Most readers of the *National Reformer* were in northeastern states like Massachusetts, New York, New Jersey, and Pennsylvania. When Whipper's society closed, the magazine ceased publication.

Freedom, and *Herald of Freedom*, openly stated these goals. These antebellum papers linked a scattered black community. They also fed growing support against slavery.

The antebellum black press often struggled to pay for printing. Most of the press's money came from subscriptions. They also appealed to white sympathizers and successful free blacks for donations. Sometimes, publishers used their personal money to keep the press in business.

Publishers of a black paper hoped the paper would bring in enough money to support printing. They also hoped for the bare minimum to support their families. If the press could not pay enough, editors held other jobs as ministers, doctors, and speakers.

Samuel Ringgold Ward, founder of Syracuse's *Impartial Citizen*, wrote about his financial struggle:

> No Anti-Slavery paper has ever yet supported an editor, unless it was endowed richly . . . no man of common sense will expect to live upon the income of a dollar paper, having but

> 1,500 subscribers when the bare expense of publishing must use up almost the whole of that sum. Let them remember that while they [readers] can easily find fault, the editor working with all his might can hardly find bread.[18]

Despite publisher efforts, money problems forced most antebellum papers to close within a year. The number of free, educated blacks who bought papers was small. Very few whites read black papers. Without enough subscribers, many papers did not have enough money to keep printing.

New York's "Colored Clause"

Before the Civil War, New York State was a hotbed for civil rights issues. It was also a popular place for the black press. More than half of the antebellum papers published were in New York. The story of how one New York paper, the *Ram's Horn*, got its start was typical of many black papers of this time.

In an effort to limit black voting rights, the New York state legislature had approved a "colored clause." The clause required black men to own $250 in real estate and have paid all back taxes

The white paper, the *New York Sun*, encouraged whites to vote "no" for black voting rights.

Mary Ann Shadd Cary

Mary Ann Shadd Cary is considered the first black female journalist in North America. She was born in 1823 in Delaware to free abolitionist parents. As a young woman Cary taught in schools for black children. She also shared her antislavery views in newspapers like Frederick Douglass's *North Star*.

In 1850 the Fugitive Slave Act allowed free blacks and fugitive slaves to be sent back to the South. Not feeling safe, Cary moved to Canada. In 1853 she founded her own weekly newspaper, the *Provincial Freeman*. In her paper Cary protested slavery. She also encouraged blacks to move to Canada, where she believed they would find more freedom and opportunity. "You have a right to your freedom and to every other privilege connected with it and if you cannot secure these in Virginia or Alabama, by all means make your escape without delay to some other locality in God's wide universe," Cary wrote.

After the Civil War, Cary returned to the United States and became the country's first black female lawyer. Until her death in 1893, Cary continued to fight for black and women's rights.

Quoted in Black History Pages, "Mary Ann Shadd Cary." http://blackhistorypages.net/pages/mashadd.php.

Journalist Mary Ann Shadd Cary.

before they could vote. White men did not have these conditions to vote. They only had to be twenty years old.

The black community and civil rights activists protested the unfair clause. After their protests the New York legislature put the issue before voters in 1846. One popular white paper, the *New York Sun*, encouraged its readers to support the clause. *Sun* editors asked whites to vote "no" for black voting rights.

Unfair Treatment by the White Press

At the time Willis Hodges was a free black living in New York. Angered by the *Sun's* position, he wrote a rebuttal editorial and sent it to the paper. To have his editorial published, the *Sun* charged Hodges fifteen dollars, a huge amount of money at the time. If Hodges had been white, the paper would have printed his editorial for free. When the *Sun* did print Hodges's editorial, they made many changes to it. They also printed it as an advertisement instead of an editorial.

Hodges went to the *Sun's* offices to protest their treatment of his writing. While he was there, one editor told him, "*The Sun* shines for all white men, not black men. You must get up a paper of your own if you want to tell your side of the story to the public."[19]

Hodges was frustrated by his treatment at the *Sun*. Even worse, he had nowhere to voice his frustrations. After *Rights for All* and the *Colored American* closed, there were no black papers in print in New York City. That made Hodges think about starting his own paper. "These cool remarks of the *Sun's* editor set me a-thinking. All the papers of note that a few years before were fighting the battles of the oppressed man of color, were now either dead or sleeping, so the idea struck me that the editor of the *Sun* was not far from right after all,"[20] he wrote.

Raising Money for a New Paper

Hodges made a living by selling items like eggs, butter, and chickens from a market stall. If he wanted to start his own press, however, he would need more money. "Now white washing was a good business. So I put a nephew in charge of the stall in the market and worked at the white washing business every day except Sundays, when I would stay and sell in the market,"[21] Hodges wrote.

After a few months Hodges earned enough money to print his paper. The first issue of the *Ram's Horn* appeared on January 1, 1847. Hodges hired his friend, Thomas Van Rensselaer, as coeditor of the paper. Rensselaer was a runaway slave who had become a well-known black abolitionist. Hodges also hired another rising black leader, Frederick Douglass, as a contributor.

On that first day Hodges's hopes were high for his new press. In the paper's prospectus, Hodges wrote, "We hope, like Joshua of old, to blow 'The Ram's Horn' until the walls of slavery and injustice fall."[22] The paper reached a circulation peak of twenty-five hundred subscribers. Unfortunately, the paper lasted less than two years. In 1848 a disagreement between Hodges and Rensselaer caused a rift between the partners. After eighteen months Hodges resigned from the paper. Rensselaer published one more issue and then closed the *Ram's Horn*.

Frederick Douglass's Rising Star

Near the end of the *Ram's Horn*, another paper began in Rochester, New York. Frederick Douglass was a rising abolitionist star. He knew the black press could be used as a weapon to fight for black rights. Douglass wrote:

> The grand thing to be done, therefore, was to change the estimation in which the colored people of the U.S. were held; to remove the prejudice which depreciated and depressed them; to prove them worthy of a higher consideration; to disprove their alleged inferiority, and demonstrate their capacity for a more exalted civilization than salary and prejudice had assigned to them.[23]

Frederick Douglass was a respected abolitionist who lectured often and started the *North Star* newspaper.

THE NORTH STAR.

ROCHESTER, N. Y., FRIDAY, JUNE 2, 1848.

The first issue of the *North Star* was released in 1847. Along with the black community, presidents and congressmen read the paper.

He took his case to England, where his English friends gave him more than two thousand dollars to start his paper.

Douglass was determined that his paper would succeed where other black papers had failed. He knew many papers had closed because they did not have enough money or experience. For his paper Douglass turned to experienced men. He hired Martin Delany from the *Pittsburgh Mystery* newspaper as coeditor. Delany's *Mystery* had been widely read for five years. Douglass also brought William C. Nell, an author and activist, on board as the publisher. Douglass spent hours with Delany and Nell talking about important details like content, design, distribution, and fund-raising. He wanted to learn from earlier papers' mistakes.

The *North Star*

The first issue of Douglass's paper, the *North Star,* appeared on December 3, 1847. He named the weekly paper after the North Star that escaping slaves followed to freedom. The motto of the paper was "Right is of No Sex—Truth is of No Color—God is the Father of Us All, And All We Are Brethren."[24] It stated Douglass's beliefs in equal rights for all, no matter if one was black or white, man or woman.

Like many white abolitionist papers, the *North Star*'s front page featured news about slavery. The rest of the paper was similar to other black newspapers. Each issue had reports from distant black communities. It also ran book reviews, fiction, verse, and editorials.

Douglass's hard work turned the *North Star* into a success. His paper marked the beginning of journalistic excellence for the black press. It was widely read and boasted more than four thousand subscribers at its height. Readers respected Douglass and the paper's messages. The *North Star*'s influence even reached beyond the black community. Presidents, senators, and congressmen read Douglass's paper.

Still, the *North Star* had its share of problems. Antiblack groups sometimes violently opposed the paper. At times Douglass struggled to find qualified staff to work on the paper. Like other editors at black presses, he always searched for money to support the paper. Sometimes Douglass added extra lectures to his schedule to earn money for the paper. Other times white supporter Julia Griffiths raised funds through bazaars and benefits. One time Douglass even mortgaged his home to keep printing the paper.

Merging to Survive

Eventually, the *North Star* grew desperate for money. In 1851 Douglass merged his paper with white abolitionist Gerrit Smith's *Liberty Party Paper*. The combined paper was called *Frederick Douglass' Paper*. Its first issue hit the streets on June 26, 1851. By 1856, however, the paper had run up debts of fifteen hundred dollars. Douglass and Smith worked to keep the paper alive in spite of their money troubles. Eventually, however, the paper closed in 1863.

The *North Star* and its successor, *Frederick Douglass' Paper*, would be remembered as some of the most influential papers before the Civil War. Many readers were white. The constant quality of Douglass's work proved to them that blacks were not born inferior to whites. White abolitionist William Lloyd Garrison called the *North Star* one of the country's best literary journals.

The *North Star* raised the standards for future papers. Douglass had shown how to keep a black paper in business for more than fifteen years. He also demonstrated the value of excellent writing and design. The *North Star* encouraged and inspired other black editors and journalists that would follow in the years to come.

Frederick Douglass

Many consider Frederick Douglass to be the father of the civil rights movement. Douglass was born a slave in Tuckahoe, Maryland. After enduring years of brutal treatment, Douglass escaped to Massachusetts in 1838. Once free Douglass discovered his talent for delivering speeches. He traveled the North giving lectures for the American Anti-Slavery Society. One listener described reactions to Douglass's speeches: "Flinty hearts were pierced, and cold ones melted by his eloquence."

Douglass also worked with the Underground Railroad, helping slaves escape to the North. He published his autobiography, *Narrative of the Life of Frederick Douglass, an American Slave, Written by Himself*, in 1845. Three years later he would publish the first issue of the *North Star*. It would become one of the most influential black newspapers during the antebellum years.

During the Civil War, Douglass acted as an adviser to President Abraham Lincoln. He fought for constitutional amendments that would establish voting and civil rights for blacks. Until his death in 1895, Douglass was a powerful and influential force in the fight for civil rights.

Quoted in Africans in America, "People & Events: Frederick Douglass," PBS. www.pbs.org/wgbh/aia/part4/4p1539.html.

The Black Press Spreads West

In the 1840s and 1850s, debate over slavery grew more intense. Abolitionists and free blacks called for slavery's end. They challenged fugitive slave laws. Some even accepted violence as a way to freedom.

Many northern whites also grew sympathetic to calls to end slavery. By 1850 northern antislavery groups swelled over 150,000 members. Senator John C. Calhoun of South Carolina predicted the nation was heading for war. In a Senate speech he said: "The agitation has been permitted to proceed, with almost no attempt to resist it, until it has reached a period when it can no longer be disguised or denied that the Union is in danger. . . . If something decisive is not done to arrest it, the South will be forced to choose between abolition and secession."[25]

During these years the black press spread west. Until then black newspapers existed mainly in eastern cities. Now the rising stars of the antislavery movement traveled west. They brought the idea of the black press with them. These journalists were often doctors, businessmen, or ministers. They were also skilled speakers and writers. As they moved into western territories, they opened new papers to protest the issues of slavery and black rights. Soon states as far west as Utah and California had black papers.

Black Press in the South

In 1861 Abraham Lincoln became the president of the United States. Almost immediately, several southern states seceded from the Union. On April 12, 1861, a young rebel commander gave the order to open fire on Fort Sumter, South Carolina. The Civil War had begun. Over the next four years, the North and South would battle in a bloody, bitter war.

During this time, a small community of free blacks lived in the South. They were free people from the Caribbean and Atlantic islands. In New Orleans a group of free black men decided to form their own press. *L'Union* became the first black paper in the South. Its debut issue appeared in September 1862. The paper was printed weekly in French but eventually added an English section.

L'Union marked a change in the black press. It moved from trying to free slaves to helping blacks establish a community. It also tried to educate blacks to survive in a free society. Unfortunately, printing the paper in French caused problems. Most readers did not speak French. In 1864 *L'Union* printed its last issue.

After *L'Union* closed, one of its founders, Louis C. Roudanez, bought the printing equipment. Two days later he launched *La Tribune de La Nouvelle-Orleans* or the *New Orleans Tribune*. It began as a triweekly paper but quickly switched to a daily paper. Printing issues six days a week, the *Tribune* became the black press's first daily paper. During its five-year run, the *Tribune* called for black rights and awakened blacks to the importance of the right to vote.

On April 9, 1865, General Robert E. Lee surrendered his Confederate forces to Union general Ulysses S. Grant. After four long years the war was over. Freedom from slavery brought high hopes for the black community. It also brought new challenges for the black press.

Chapter Three

The Black Press and Reconstruction

The end of the Civil War brought hope for the future to the black community. After years of struggle and protest, southern slavery had ended. Optimism reigned. On April 15, 1865, an editorial in the *Black Republican* said:

> The dark clouds that hung over us; the chains [that] bound us; the prisons, whose very walls re-echoed our lamentations as we sent them up to heaven—these have all passed away; a river of blood has passed on with a mighty current, carrying the accursed things out of the world. Better times have come. We live in brighter days. The sun shines and the blessed rain of heaven is falling.[26]

Freedom to Read

For many slaves reading was one of the sweetest gifts of freedom. White slaveholders had forbidden slaves to read. They feared slaves who could read would communicate with each other and organize revolts. In the slaveholding South many states even passed legislation that forbade slaves from reading.

Now blacks could read without fear of punishment. For many the black press was their first introduction to the written

Freed slaves learn to read in a schoolroom in 1866. Most slaves had been forbidden to read by slaveholders.

word. Booker T. Washington, a former slave who would become a leader in the black community, wrote about the newly discovered passion for reading.

> I can recall vividly the picture not only of children, but of men and women, some of whom had reached the age of sixty or seventy, tramping along the country roads with a spelling book or a Bible in their hands. It did not seem to

> occur to anyone that age was any obstacle to learning in books. With weak and unaccustomed eyes, old men and old women would struggle along month after month in their effort to master the primer.[27]

Reconstruction Begins

After the initial excitement over the war's end, the reality of the situation became clear. Approximately 4 million slaves were now free people. Most of them, however, were poor and illiterate. Many were also homeless after being thrown off slaveholders' lands. The newly freed slaves had few skills or resources to survive independently. Also, war had devastated the southern lands. Much work would be needed to repair and rebuild towns.

Forbidden to Read

In the South white slaveholders feared that reading would help black slaves gather and rise up against their owners. Many communities passed laws that made it illegal for slaves to read. Being caught with a black newspaper could also bring severe punishment. One North Carolina law stated:

> Whereas the teaching of slaves to read and write, has a tendency to excite dissatisfaction in their minds, and to produce insurrection and rebellion, to the manifest injury of the citizens of this State: Therefore be it enacted by the General Assembly of the State of North Carolina . . . that any free person, who shall hereafter teach or attempt to teach, any slave within the State to read or write . . . upon conviction shall, at the discretion of the court, if a white man or woman, be fined not less than one hundred dollars, or imprisoned; and if a free person of color, shall be fined, imprisoned or whipped, at the discretion of the court, not exceeding thirty-nine lashes, nor less than twenty lashes.

Quoted in Armistead S. Pride and Clint C. Wilson II, *A History of the Black Press*. Washington, DC: Howard University Press, 1997, p. 76.

There was a boom in the black press after the Civil War. Even tiny towns wanted their own printing press.

Building a Community

The end of the war unleashed a burst of energy in the black press. Newly freed slaves wanted to communicate and connect with each other. The black press stepped into that role. Between the end of the Civil War and the 1890s, more than five hundred black presses began printing across the country. Even tiny towns wanted their own press. Some borrowed printing presses from black churches to print their papers.

Many papers only lasted a few months or years. However, they accomplished an enormous task. After the war the black press pulled former slaves and free blacks together into a community. The papers helped build hope and morale. They told blacks about community news and built a sense of racial identity. In the New Orleans *Black Republican*, an editorial read: "Honesty, industry, temperance, religion, education, truthfulness—these will be the virtues that will make us strong; and then let us be strong by our unity, our harmony among ourselves. . . . There is yet much that we can attain."[28]

The black press recognized the importance of education. At the war's end many freed slaves were illiterate. They would have to learn basic skills like reading and writing to survive and contribute to society. Northern aid groups helped create southern black schools. Black communities themselves banded together to hire teachers and find buildings for schools. Black editors wrote articles to encourage blacks to take advantage of these new opportunities to learn. An editorial in the *New York Globe* stated, "There was never a time when education effort was more needed in the south than at the present—education that will prepare the boy and girl for the serious duties of manhood and womanhood."[29]

Congressional Actions

Abraham Lincoln's Emancipation Proclamation had freed the slaves, but it did not grant basic rights. To correct this situation, the federal government passed three constitutional Amendments after the Civil War.

In 1865 the Thirteenth Amendment formally abolished slavery across the United States. In 1868 the Fourteenth Amendment gave blacks full citizenship and equal protection under the law. The Fourteenth Amendment states:

> All persons born or naturalized in the United States, and subject to the jurisdiction thereof, are citizens of the United States and of the State wherein they reside. No State shall make or enforce any law which shall abridge the privileges

> or immunities of citizens of the United States; nor shall any State deprive any person of life, liberty, or property, without due process of law; nor deny to any person within its jurisdiction the equal protection of the laws.[30]

The Fifteenth Amendment, ratified in 1870, made it illegal for states to deny citizens the right to vote based on race.

In addition to the constitutional amendments, Congress also issued the Civil Rights Act of 1866. It gave former slaves a variety of civil rights, including the right to own property, be heard in court, and enter into contracts.

Unfortunately, these federal laws had little impact on the daily life of southern blacks. Southern whites still held a deep resentment against the black community. Blacks hoped freedom and Reconstruction would bring equality. Southern whites were determined to make sure that did not happen.

Black Codes and Southern Restrictions

After the war many southern whites returned to their old ways. The slaves might be free, but whites still treated them as inferior beings. Around 1865 many southern states started passing laws known as Black Codes. These laws limited the freedom of blacks. They restricted where blacks could work and live and even who they could marry.

The Civil Rights Act of 1866 tried to overrule the Black Codes. Unfortunately, whites controlled the southern police, courts, and legislatures. They intimidated blacks from even trying to assert their legal rights. Too often, if a former slave brought a complaint to the court, the case was simply ignored.

The southern states also tried to restrict black voting rights by adding understanding clauses to their voting laws. These clauses required blacks to read and understand the Constitution before they could vote. Good conduct clauses also denied voting rights if a black man had been arrested for any minor offense.

Hostility Increases

As the black press worked hard to elevate the black community, southern whites became more hostile. They tried even harder to repress blacks. White papers joined in the repression efforts.

Southern whites grew more hostile and groups like the Ku Klux Klan formed and backlashed against the black press.

They printed editorials from angry whites who complained about blacks and claimed they were inferior to whites.

As hostility rose, violence against blacks also increased. White mobs beat blacks and destroyed their property for minor offenses. Kidnappings, murders, and lynchings were common. During this time secret organized groups like the Ku Klux Klan formed. They terrorized blacks to keep them from challenging white power.

In 1877 President Rutherford B. Hayes withdrew federal troops from the South. During the Civil War, Union troops had slowly occupied the southern states. They remained after the war to oversee Reconstruction in the South. They also dealt with local violence and enforced civil rights legislation.

When the troops left, the black community was left vulnerable. Southern whites were angry over losing the war and their slaves. Many times their anger turned into violence. They destroyed black property and schools. They also beat and lynched blacks. Groups like the Ku Klux Klan often organized the terror. Each year these acts grew more common.

Jim Crow Laws

After the federal troops left, former slaveholding white southerners returned to power in state and local government. Almost immediately, they passed laws to segregate the races. These laws were called Jim Crow laws, named after a black cartoon character. While Jim Crow laws differed in each state, they shared similar characteristics. Jim Crow laws restricted where blacks could live, go to school, and worship. They

A bus driver holds a sign instructing blacks to sit separately from whites. Segregation was supported by the Jim Crow laws.

required blacks to use separate public facilities. The laws also limited which jobs blacks could take. Like the earlier Black Codes, Jim Crow laws tried to block blacks from voting through literacy tests or taxes.

Some Jim Crow laws forced blacks to act subserviently to whites. Blacks had to tip their hats to whites as they passed on the street. They were expected to step out of the way for whites on the sidewalk. In stores black customers had to wait patiently to be served after whites, if they were served at all. Blacks also had to address whites with respectful titles like "sir" and "ma'am." Whites, on the other hand, called adult blacks "boy" and "girl." Even worse, many whites simply called them "n-----."

Walking a Fine Line

The black press in the South discovered that existing in this environment was a tricky task. The editors had to walk a fine line. They wanted to be fair to their black readers by reporting news and injustices. But they also needed to avoid angering hostile

Women Journalists

After Reconstruction the number of black women journalists slowly increased. Women like Cordelia Ray, Sarah Thompson, Victoria Earle Matthews, and Lucy Wilmot Smith worked as writers and editors for black newspapers and magazines. One journalist, Nellie F. Mossell, wrote for Philadelphia papers and edited the women's department of T. Thomas Fortune's *New York Freeman*. Mossell recognized the expanding opportunities for black women in journalism in the late nineteenth century. In her book titled *The Work of the Afro-American Woman*, she included a chapter about women in journalism. She wrote, "There was a day when an Afro-American woman of the greatest refinement and culture could aspire no higher than the dressmaker's art, or later . . . a teacher." The rise of the black press offered another option for these women.

Quoted in Armistead S. Pride and Clint C. Wilson II, *A History of the Black Press*. Washington, DC: Howard University Press, 1997, p. 91.

white mobs. If black editors criticized local leaders too much, they risked their lives and property.

In response many southern black papers took a less militant tone than their northern peers. Southern editors often did not write about local issues. Instead they wrote about issues outside their state or even outside the South. Black papers that did not adopt this muted approach usually did not survive.

Speaking Out in the North

The northern black press had more freedom to protest. These papers wrote about lynchings, race riots, and other injustices that occurred daily in the South. Reports from black papers served as a balance to the often biased reports that appeared in white papers. Papers like the *Chicago Conservator* (1878) and the *New York Age* (1887) became known for their bold calls for equality and justice. Wrote black journalist T. Thomas Fortune in New York's *Globe*:

> The question of the illegal suppression of a tremendous voting population is not a race question; it is a national question, defined minutely in the federal constitution. . . . A people invite destruction or violent contention by permitting fundamental laws to be abused, by permitting common rights to be usurped by an arrogant and violent class. The people of the United States will find all too soon that they are playing on top of a volcano which is liable to erupt at any moment.[31]

The Princess of the Press

Despite the risks, some southern black editors refused to tone down their papers and protests. One editor, Ida B. Wells, became known as the Princess of the Press. The daughter of slave parents, Ida spent hours reading the local black paper to her father. As a young woman she contributed articles to several presses. In 1889 Wells joined a new weekly paper in Tennessee, the *Memphis Free Speech and Headlight*, as editor and part owner.

In the *Free Speech*, Wells spoke out aggressively against injustice. She ran a series of exposés on local school boards and attacked the voter understanding clauses. Her bold and militant style attracted readers. Subscriptions quickly jumped from fifteen

SOUTHERN HORRORS.

LYNCH LAW

IN ALL

ITS PHASES

Miss IDA B. WELLS,

Price, - - - Fifteen Cents.

THE NEW YORK AGE PRINT,

1892.

Ida B. Wells aggressively spoke out against lynching.

hundred to four thousand, and the paper spread from Tennessee to neighboring southern states.

Wells Opposes Lynching

Of all injustices, Wells especially hated lynching. White mobs in the South lynched blacks without fear of punishment from law enforcement. White leaders claimed lynchings for serious crimes like rape and murder were justified. White Memphis papers also supported lynching. They wrote that lynch mobs were "a violent but necessary abrogation of civil law in cases involving rape."[32]

In 1892 racial tensions rose in Memphis. Three of Wells's friends were lynched after defending their grocery store from white attackers. Wells suggested that white grocers called for the attack to eliminate the competition. She wrote in the *Free Speech*:

> The city of Memphis has demonstrated that neither character nor standing avails the Negro if he dares to protect himself against the white man or become his rival. There is nothing we can do about the lynching now, as we are outnumbered and without arms. The white mob could help itself to ammunition without pay, but the order is rigidly enforced against the selling of guns to Negroes. There is therefore only one thing left to do; save our money and leave a town which will neither protect our lives and property, nor give us a fair trial in the courts, but takes us out and murders us in cold blood when accused by white persons.[33]

Many black families took Wells's advice: They fled Memphis for Oklahoma. Others did not buy from white businesses. White officials warned Wells to stop publishing her critical articles. Wells refused and continued to publish accounts of injustice and attacks on blacks.

Wells also launched an investigation into local lynchings. Officials claimed that lynchings were used to punish serious crimes. Wells found that less than 25 percent of lynched blacks were accused of rape. Many more lynchings happened because of minor offenses. Some were lynched for insulting whites or not stepping aside when a white person passed. Using her findings, Wells wrote militant editorials to challenge Memphis officials.

In one editorial Wells even suggested that white women were not completely innocent in alleged rape cases. "It is a sacred convention that white women can never feel passion of any sort, high or low, for a black man. Unfortunately, sex don't always square with the convention. And then if the guilty pair are found out, the thing is christened in outrage at once and the woman is practically forced to join in hounding down the partner of her shame."[34]

It was the first time a black editor had dared to say such a thing. Two white papers immediately attacked Wells. They wrote that whites had suffered "the ultimate indignity, and . . . were compelled to insure the heresy would never be repeated."[35]

Facing Danger

Wells realized that her life was in danger from angry whites. She bought a gun and carried it with her. "I felt that one had better die fighting against injustice than to die like a dog or a rat in a trap. I had already determined to sell my life as dearly as possible if attacked. I felt if I could take one lyncher with me, this would even up the score a little bit."[36]

When the mob did attack, however, Wells was out of town. On May 27, 1892, a group of whites gathered at the *Free Speech* offices. They ran the paper's business manager out of town and then destroyed the office and printing equipment. The mob also left a note, threatening death to anyone who tried to publish the paper again. This violent response served as a warning for southern black editors to be careful with their words.

Wells received the news about her paper's destruction while she was meeting with another black editor, T. Thomas Fortune. He immediately offered her a position with his paper, the *New York Age*. Wells realized that she could not return to the South or she would be killed by the mob. She decided to take the job with Fortune's paper to "continue my fight against lynching and lynchers. They had destroyed my paper, in which every dollar I had in the world was invested. They had made me an exile and threatened my life for hinting at the truth. I felt that I owed it to myself and my race to tell the whole truth."[37] In return for the *Free Speech*'s subscription list, Wells became part owner of the *Age*.

She continued to write biting attacks on injustice in the South, especially lynchings.

A Crusader in the North

In the 1870s white papers regularly printed stereotypes of blacks. They openly supported racism and the belief that blacks were inferior to whites. As the white papers stepped up their smear campaigns, the young black journalist T. Thomas Fortune began to make a name for himself. He wrote editorials against racism and the treatment of blacks in the white press. His harsh criticisms appealed to readers around the country.

Born a slave in Florida, Fortune began his newspaper career as an errand boy for several southern white newspapers. In 1881 he moved to New York City. He wrote and set type for a black weekly called the *Globe*.

The *Globe* became well known for top-notch news coverage and writing. Whites and blacks read the paper for reliable Negro news and opinion. At the *Globe* Fortune became a skilled editorial writer. His militant editorials attracted readers and built his name in the journalism community. He often called for blacks to resist white oppression. On November 10, 1883, Fortune wrote:

> There is but one way to put a period to the force and violence of Bourbon [southern Democrat]—use more force and violence than he uses. As he believes in brute force, he respect[s] it, even when it [is] used by those he hates and stabs in the dark. . . . Let the colored man stand his ground. There is far more honor in dying like a free man than living like a slave.[38]

These militant writings caused the white press to label Fortune as an agitator.

Fortune Opens the *New York Freeman*

The *Globe* closed in November 1884 because of financial troubles. Fortune decided to open his own paper, and two weeks later he printed the first issue of the *New York Freeman*.

At the *Freeman* Fortune became known as the best black journalist of the time. The paper carried Fortune's militant and independent style. It called for blacks to defend themselves

Charlotta Bass

Born in 1874, Charlotta Bass became one of the most influential black journalists and activists of her time. In 1912 she took over the *California Eagle* as managing editor and publisher. Founded in 1879, the *Eagle* was one of the longest-running black papers. Bass used the *Eagle* to push for reforms in the black community.

Bass was well known for her outspoken style and radical views. She openly criticized the housing authority, the real estate association, and the police force. She also protested the 1915 film *Birth of a Nation*, which showed the Ku Klux Kan in a favorable light. "We of the *Eagle* pioneered in an important field of social struggle, the struggle to make the film industry responsible morally for the content of its products," she wrote.

Bass's blunt style earned her death threats on several occasions. Her criticism of the U.S. government also branded her a troublemaker and suspected Communist. The post office investigated Bass and revoked the *Eagle*'s mailing privileges. The FBI followed her and read her mail. These obstacles did not stop Bass, however. Even after her retirement from the newspaper in 1951, Bass continued working for civil and political rights for the black community.

Quoted in PBS, *The Black Press: Soldiers Without Swords*. www.pbs.org/ blackpress/film/index.html.

Influential journalist Charlotta Bass.

against white aggression. On July 18, 1885, a *Freeman* editorial said:

> Colored men of the South, turn on the light! . . . It is a reproach and an insult to our manhood that we allow ourselves to be shot, outraged and lynched without one word of protest, or the uplifting of a finger in self-defense. Stand up for your rights, and if they be denied you by the courts of law, defend yourselves with the same arguments used to outrage you. What is fair for the one is fair for the other, and if the white scamps lynch and shoot you, you have a right to do the same.[39]

In 1887 the paper was renamed the *New York Age*. After a brief absence from the paper, Fortune returned as *Age*'s editor. He still wrote sharp editorials on racial issues. His reputation for having a sharp pen became widely known. Even Theodore Roosevelt is reported to have said, "Tom Fortune, for God's sake, keep that pen of yours off me."[40]

Signs of Change

After the Civil War the black press slowly changed. Papers no longer needed antislavery articles. They replaced them with articles on science, art, literature, and drama. The papers also spread further around the country. By the end of the nineteenth century, there were black papers in most states.

Black papers also found new readers and sources of money. Former slaves learning to read opened up a larger audience. Free men earning money were able to pay for subscriptions. Social services and religious groups supported black papers. Political groups also supported papers, hoping to gain black voter support. Many papers still only lasted a short time, but now more published for longer periods.

Despite changes, the press was still a champion of rights for the black community. Slaves were free, but lynchings and segregation were a part of daily life. The fight was just beginning. In the coming years, the black press would play a vital role in the struggle for civil rights.

Chapter Four

The Increasing Power of the Press

By the late 1800s conditions for blacks were steadily getting worse. The Jim Crow era brought increased discrimination, lynching, and mob violence. Black citizens were regularly deprived of their rights and treated as second-class citizens. Instead of helping the black community, the federal government turned a blind eye to the treatment of blacks in the South.

Segregation was also on the rise. In 1883 the Supreme Court overturned the Civil Rights Act of 1875 that forbade discrimination in hotels, trains, and other public places. Then in 1896 the Supreme Court ruled in *Plessy v. Ferguson* to uphold "separate but equal" laws.

The black press became more intense during the early 1900s, as segregation and discrimination increased across the country.

This decision said that it was acceptable to have separate facilities for the races. As a result, many communities segregated virtually all areas of public life. Blacks and whites had separate schools, restrooms, theaters, and restaurants. Unfortunately, the separate facilities were rarely equal. The areas set aside for blacks were usually inferior to those for whites.

Gaining a Deeper Foothold

In this hostile environment the black press exploded. Between 1895 and 1915 more than a thousand black newspapers printed issues. Once again these papers became the voice of the black community. They protested the increasingly unjust treatment of blacks by whites. Papers like the *Colored Citizen* in Kansas spoke out against segregation and discrimination:

> All the children in the city are at liberty to attend the school nearest them, except the poor child that God for some reason chose to create with a black face instead of a white one. Our board of education . . . persist in keeping up race distinction. . . . We say to every colored man and woman in the city to come together and resolve that you will no longer submit to unjust discrimination on account of your color. This thing has gone on long enough and now if it can be stopped, let's stop it.[41]

Protesting Lynching

It is no coincidence that the increase in black newspapers at the turn of the century happened at the same time as the rise in lynchings. The years between 1881 and 1939 were known as the lynching era. Mobs lynched thousands during this time. For years lynch mobs had strung up white criminals. In the years after Reconstruction, however, more blacks fell victim to lynching. By 1900 blacks were the majority of lynching deaths.

Black editors hoped their reporting of lynchings would increase national awareness of the crimes. They provided details that the biased white newspapers did not report. They also criticized local officials for not punishing white lynch mobs.

Without protection from law enforcement, editors encouraged blacks to protect themselves. On April 9, 1887, the *Weekly Pelican* in New Orleans ran an article that stated:

> The lynching of five men at Yorkville, S.C. . . . by armed men is but another heinous crime which, from time to time, have been practiced upon the Negro. Even the judge on the bench, in instructing the Grand Jury, said that "It was [the lynching] one of those things which the law could not reach, and therefore it would be useless for them to lose their time in attempting to ferret out the perpetrators." Well, if the law can't reach the rascals, if justice can't overtake the ruthless slayers of black men and women, the only recourse the colored man has is to protect himself and to remember the old law, "an eye for an eye, and a tooth for a tooth."[42]

Division in the Black Community

As violence and discrimination increased, black leaders realized the situation was quickly getting out of control. They agreed that all people should be treated as equal citizens. All should have the same voting, social, and economic rights. They disagreed, however, on

Separate but Equal

On June 7, 1892, Homer Plessy bought a first-class train ticket to Louisiana. Under the Louisiana Separate Car Act of 1890, Plessy was banned from the white-only section because he was of mixed race. He sat in the forbidden coach and refused to move until police arrested him.

A legal battle followed. Plessy's lawyers argued that the Separate Car Act violated Plessy's rights under the Constitution. The Fourteenth Amendment stated that states could not make any law that violated the rights and privileges of U.S. citizens.

The case, *Plessy v. Ferguson*, eventually landed before the U.S. Supreme Court in 1896. After deliberation the Court ruled 8 to 1 that the concept of *separate but equal* was acceptable under the Constitution.

The aftermath of the ruling led to "separate but equal" facilities in most public areas. The unfortunate reality, however, was that black facilities were usually inferior to white-only areas.

how to reach those goals. Some believed blacks should accommodate whites and wait patiently for their rights. Others felt that they should fight now for equal treatment. As the disagreement grew more bitter, it played out on the pages of the black press.

Booker T. Washington's Message of Accommodation

Booker T. Washington was one of the most powerful black leaders at the end of the nineteenth century. He strongly believed that pushing too hard for equality would jeopardize the future of blacks in America. Washington argued that blacks should try to accommodate and get along with whites. Instead of fighting for

Booker T. Washington's famous speeches helped make him one of the most powerful black leaders at the end of the nineteenth century.

civil rights, blacks should focus on improving themselves first. If they worked hard in valuable jobs and became important to the economy, Washington believed blacks would eventually gain equal rights. Washington wanted blacks to be patient while they waited to "earn" their rights.

In 1895 Washington spoke at the Cotton States and International Exposition in Atlanta. In his famous speech he criticized those who pushed too quickly for equality:

> Our greatest danger is that in the great leap from slavery to freedom, we may overlook the fact that the masses of us are to live by the productions of our hands and fail to keep in our mind that we shall prosper in proportion as we learn to dignify and glorify common labor. . . . It is at the bottom of life we should begin and not the top. Nor should we let our grievances overshadow our opportunities.

Then Washington held his hand high over his head and spread his fingers apart. "In all things that are purely social we can be as separate as the finger yet one as the hand in all things essential to mutual progress."[43]

The white press lauded Washington's speech. Political leaders, including President Grover Cleveland, congratulated him. Many hoped race relations had turned a new, less violent page.

Washington's Influence in the Press

Washington's money and power helped him spread his views in black newspapers. Black papers still struggled to survive with low circulation. Many still relied on contributions from men like Washington to stay in business.

Washington secretly gave several papers money in exchange for printing editorials that supported his views. If Washington could not influence a paper, he sometimes tried to run it out of business by supporting its direct competitor. Historian Edgar A. Toppin wrote about Washington's methods:

> The Tuskegee [Washington's] news bureau . . . sent out a flood of news releases and canned editorials. By placing or withholding ads, the well-endowed Tuskegee clique persuaded many black editors, most of whose publications were in financial straits, to carry these materials favorable to Washington's views. Moreover, the Tuskegee cabal secretly purchased several black periodicals, controlling them unbeknownst to the public.[44]

One of the papers that Washington targeted was T. Thomas Fortune's popular *New York Age*. Washington financially supported the *Age* for several years. Eventually, he purchased the paper. In return Fortune published Washington's editorials in favor of accommodation. Personally, Fortune disagreed with Washington and believed in fighting for black rights. Sometimes Fortune would write an opposing editorial and run it in the same issue as one of Washington's.

Criticism from the North

Like Fortune, not all black editors agreed with Washington's views on race relations. William Monroe Trotter was born in Massachusetts and graduated from Harvard. He followed his father into the real estate field, but the writings and speeches of Washington angered him. He said, "What man is a worse enemy

William Trotter disagreed with Booker T. Washington's views on segregation and pleaded passionately for equality for all men.

to a race than a leader who looks with equanimity on the disfranchisement of his race in a country where other races have universal suffrage by constitutions that make one rule for his race and another for the dominant race."[45]

By 1901 Trotter decided to speak out in his own paper. "The conviction grew on me that pursuit of business, money, civic or literary position was like building a house upon the sands, if race prejudice and persecution for mere color were to spread up from the South and result in a fixed cast of color,"[46] he said.

With partner George Forbes, Trotter opened a weekly paper called the *Boston Guardian*. The paper's first issue in November 1901 stated, "We have come to protest forever against being . . . shut off from equal rights with other citizens, and shall remain forever on the firing line . . . in defence of such rights."[47] Trotter thought the *Guardian*'s Boston offices were symbolic. They worked in the same building where William Lloyd Garrison's *Liberator* had been published years before.

Trotter marketed his paper to appeal to readers in New England and beyond. He included national news, social notes from the South and Midwest, church news, fashion, sports, features, and fiction. The *Guardian* became best known, however, for its editorial page. Its bitter, satirical style attracted attention from the black community across the country. On the editorial page Trotter attacked Washington and his accommodationist views on a weekly basis. In one issue Trotter criticized blacks who kept quiet about injustice. "Silence is tantamount to being virtually an accomplice in the treasonable act of this Benedict Arnold of the Negro race. O, for a black Patrick Henry to save his people from this stigma of cowardice."[48]

Trotter and Du Bois

Trotter joined forces with another rising black leader, W.E.B. Du Bois, to oppose Washington. Du Bois, also born in Massachusetts, had lost patience with the slow pace of race relations. He believed Washington's methods were not working and a more aggressive approach was needed. Together Trotter and Du Bois used the *Guardian* to speak for civil rights for all blacks. The paper's militant style was a stark contrast to the more muted tone of papers that supported Washington's views.

Trotter's *Boston Guardian* managed to stay in print until the 1950s. It had faced overwhelming odds by opposing the powerful Washington and other black papers of the time. Trotter's militant style and unwillingness to compromise on equal rights set an example for the black press in the coming twentieth century.

Abbott and the *Chicago Defender*

A few years before Trotter's paper debuted, the seeds of the most successful black newspaper were planted. In 1893 a young printing student named Robert Abbott attended Colored American Day at the Columbian Exposition in Chicago. He sat in Festival

Chicago Defender founder Robert Abbott, right, stands by his printing press.

Hall as Frederick Douglass delivered a passionate speech. Douglass's voice rumbled through the hall as he spoke, saying:

> Men talk of the "negro problem". There is no negro problem. The problem is whether the American people have honesty enough, loyalty enough, honor enough, patriotism enough to live up to their own constitution. We intend that the American people shall learn the great lesson of the brotherhood of man and the fatherhood of God from our presence among them.[49]

At the fair Abbott mingled with the leaders of the black community and became inspired by their passion.

After Abbott finished his printing studies, he returned to Chicago. Discrimination against his dark skin made finding a printing job difficult. Abbott then enrolled in law school. After graduation he was again told he was too dark to make an impact on a white judge. Frustrated, Abbott turned to journalism.

In 1905 Abbott set up his newspaper office in a rented room with a card table, a chair, and twenty-five cents. The first issue of Abbott's *Chicago Defender* appeared on March 4, 1905. In the beginning Abbott was a one-man show. He wrote, printed, and sold the papers himself. In time Abbott used agents to distribute the paper in Chicago and the Midwest. He also made a pivotal decision to send his paper into the South. Ninety percent of the black community lived in the South. And they were ready to read the *Defender*.

Sensational Headlines

In the beginning Abbott's *Defender* avoided politics. As the paper grew, Abbott studied the success of William Randolph Hearst's white newspapers. Hearst's papers used sensationalist headlines to boost sales. Abbott realized a successful paper needed to capture the attention of the largest number of readers. To do that he needed to highlight stories with the most interest for the common black man.

Previous black newspapers had targeted a small group of educated readers. They featured commentary and editorials about national news. Abbott changed that approach. He reached out to the largest audience, the common black man. To grab readers' at-

Stretching the Truth

Robert Abbott's sensational style of reporting attracted readers by the thousands to the *Chicago Defender*. The *Defender*, however, was not known for being 100 percent accurate in its reporting. "I tell the truth if I can get it, but if I can't get the facts, I read between the lines and tell what I know to be facts even though the reports say differently," explained Abbott.

Quoted in Charles A. Simmons, *The African American Press: With Special Reference to Four Newspapers, 1827–1965*. Jefferson, NC: McFarland, 1998, p. 30.

tention, Abbott designed screaming red headlines. The *Defender* ran front-page stories about crime and lurid events. It featured exposés on prostitution and other crimes in the black community. Some people criticized the *Defender*'s sensationalism. There was no denying, however, that the strategy worked.

The *Defender* attracted readers in droves. By 1910 circulation grew over one hundred thousand copies per week. The *Defender* was read aloud in homes, barber shops, street corners, and churches. Vernon Jarrett remembers the *Defender* when he was a young boy in the South:

> My grandfather, an ex-slave who was illiterate, we didn't know it at the time, made my brother, as a little boy, read the *Chicago Defender* from page to page, including the ads. And he would make him go back and say, "Read that again, boy." He wanted to hear about what was going on in different parts of the world. This was, ah, I guess my grandfather's way of realizing he was a free man, a black newspaper from Up North.[50]

With multiple readers of each issue, Abbott's *Defender* reached over a half a million blacks across the country. Within ten years it outsold every black press in the country.

Abbott's Straight Talk

Abbott used the *Defender* to raise awareness about injustice in the black community. He ran articles and editorials on lynching, segregation, and how to advance the black race. Because the *Defender*

The nationally popular *Chicago Defender* ran influential articles on lynching and how to advance the black race.

was a northern paper, Abbott was able to say things that southern black papers could not. Blacks in the south came to trust Abbott and the *Defender* for its straightforward style.

In his harsh editorials Abbott's sarcastic style was popular with readers. In one issue, he wrote:

> Fifty-four lynchings occurred in the United States during the year 1914, six more than during the preceding year. Only 49 of the 53 being colored, showing conclusively that a grievous error was made somewhere. Think of it. Five white men lynched! It seems that we can [have] nothing exclusive. Lynching was a form of punishment, especially prepared for us. At least that is what we have been led to believe. Perhaps the fun wasn't coming fast and furious enough, so they threw in a few of their own number for a good measure.[51]

Abbott also made fun of the white press's habit of putting *negro* in parentheses after a black person's name. He decided to treat white people the same way in his paper. The *Defender* would read, for example, "Woodrow Wilson (white) declared war on Germany yesterday."[52]

The popularity of the *Defender* did not escape the white community's notice. Some communities tried to prevent the paper's distribution. The Ku Klux Klan threatened blacks found with *Defender* copies. White mobs killed two *Defender* agents and drove others from their homes.

Advertising Versus Activism

Over the years many black newspapers faced the same dilemma. What was the best way to balance advertising and activism? If papers were strong activists, advertisers refused to purchase ads. But if a paper toned down their calls for equality, readers stopped reading the paper. Fewer readers led to lower advertising dollars.

Robert Abbott discovered a solution to this problem. His *Defender* appealed to the largest reader base in black newspaper history. This large base caused him to rely less on money from advertisers. He could also drop the price of his paper, which brought in even more subscribers. Because he did not depend on

Outrage at the Supreme Court

When the Supreme Court overturned the 1875 Civil Rights Act, many people were outraged. Bishop Henry McNeal Turner, an activist for black rights, said:

The world has never witnessed such barbarous laws entailed upon a free people as have grown out of the decision of the United States Supreme Court, issued October 15, 1883. For that decision alone authorized and now sustains all the unjust discriminations, proscriptions and robberies perpetrated by public carriers upon millions of the nation's most loyal defenders. It fathers all the "Jim-Crow cars" into which colored people are huddled and compelled to pay as much as the whites, who are given the finest accommodations. It has made the ballot of the black man a parody, his citizenship a nullity and his freedom a burlesque. It has engendered the bitterest feeling between the whites and blacks, and resulted in the deaths of thousands, who would have been living and enjoying life today.

Quoted in *The Rise and Fall of Jim Crow*, "Civil Rights Act of 1875 Declared Unconstitutional," PBS. www.pbs.org/wnet/jimcrow/stories_events_uncivil.html.

advertising money, Abbott could take a more militant tone in the *Defender*. This appealed to his readers and gained their loyalty.

Under this model the *Defender* became the first commercially successful black newspaper. Circulation peaked in the early 1920s at around 283,000. Abbott opened branch offices. He employed several thousand agents and correspondents to distribute the paper and gather news. When Abbott hired white employees, the *Defender* became the first integrated black paper. The *Defender*'s success made Abbott a millionaire.

The *Defender*'s reach and influence made it one of the most important and influential black newspapers in history. It would also prove instrumental as the United States entered two world wars and the Great Depression.

Chapter Five

Wartime and Depression

In 1914 World War I erupted in Europe. At first the United States stayed neutral. By 1917, however, the country entered the war and sent soldiers overseas. In wartime, northern factories boomed with orders for goods like steel and clothing. Before the war young men and European immigrants powered the factory workforce. Now the wartime draft pulled young men into military service. The war also slowed immigrant travel to the United States. Factories found themselves without enough workers. Robert Abbott and his *Defender* stepped in with a solution.

The Great Migration

Life in the South for black Americans was hard. An ongoing depression and recent losses of cotton crops to disease put many out of work. For those with jobs, wages were low. Jim Crow laws separated and humiliated them. Even worse, they risked harm to their life and property every day. Angry mobs still assaulted, lynched, and destroyed black homes and businesses.

In Chicago Robert Abbott saw the shortages World War I placed on factories like steel mills and packing houses. They needed skilled and unskilled workers. Northern factories also

paid a higher wage than southern employers. Abbott realized the time was right to help southern blacks improve their lives.

Abbott launched a major campaign to encourage southern blacks to move north. He used the *Defender* to convince southern blacks that life was better in the North. The *Defender* announced jobs and higher wages. It ran articles about better living conditions in northern cities. Abbott also ran front-page stories about southern lynchings to remind black readers about the danger

An African American family moving north. Between 1916 and 1919 approximately 500,000 blacks left the South.

they faced every day. *Defender* editorials urged blacks to migrate. One stated that

> every Negro man for the sake of his wife and daughters especially, should leave even at a financial sacrifice every spot

> in the south where his worth is not appreciated enough to give him the standing of a man and a citizen in the community. We know full well that this would almost mean a depopulation of that section and if it were possible we would glory in its accomplishment.[53]

Abbott's message struck a chord with southern blacks. Between 1916 and 1919 approximately five hundred thousand blacks left the South. They moved north and west. In the 1920s more than a million more followed. While the *Defender* received much credit for the migration, other black papers also joined in the call for blacks to move north.

Dora Harris Glasco's father was one of the many who decided to travel north. "My father read the *Chicago Defender*. It wasn't a long thing that he had to look at to see that he could benefit his children and his children's children by coming North,"[54] she said.

As they considered coming north, many black southerners wrote to Abbott thanking him and asking for information. They wrote, "I have seen your columns all about the South and the race in the North. Now I am thinking of coming this fall," and, "I like the work all right, but they don't pay enough to get myself a good hat."[55] In response Abbott printed information such as railroad timetables to Chicago in his paper.

Southern Resistance

Before long, southern whites grew alarmed at the sheer number of blacks leaving the region. The black community was vital to the southern economy. Blacks provided most of the farm and plantation labor. As thousands of blacks left, the South's economy suffered.

Southern leaders became desperate to stop the migration. Some white papers printed articles telling blacks they would freeze in the cold north. Abbott responded in the *Defender*, "If you can freeze to death in the North and be free, why freeze to death in the South and be a slave, where your mother, sister and daughter are raped and burned at the stake, where your father, brother and son are treated with contempt and hung to a pole, riddled with bullets at the least mention that he does not like the way he has been treated."[56]

As blacks continued to leave, southern towns tried new tactics. They banned the sale of black newspapers, especially the *Defender*. Ku Klux Klan members threatened anyone caught with the *Defender*.

Black railroad porters like these would hide black newspapers on trains and get them to farmworkers and those outside the city.

When Abbott could no longer sell papers through regular agents, he turned to the railroad. Black porters and railroad workers hid newspaper bundles on trains traveling south. In between towns the porters tossed the papers off the train into the countryside. Despite the efforts of southern cities, they could not stop black newspapers coming into town.

The Black Soldier

With the country at war, black newspapers faced a new dilemma. The country was fighting for democracy in Europe but still allowing Jim Crow laws to deprive blacks of voting rights at home. Many asked why blacks should support the war. Why give the lives of black soldiers to a country that did not take care of its own citizens? Still, black editors supported the war effort and encouraged black men to enlist in the army.

In the military, blacks faced the same discrimination they found at home. They could not serve in the marines. They were limited to menial positions in the navy and coast guard. Most blacks were assigned to labor battalions. Those allowed in combat units were segregated. In camp, blacks faced hostility from white soldiers. Some camps gave black soldiers inferior uniforms and sleeping quarters.

Although they supported the war, black editors protested discrimination in the military. Many editors wrote articles about the unfair treatment of black soldiers. These critical articles made the government uneasy. Some viewed newspaper attacks against the military as being disloyal to the country. Others thought it would be better to put aside differences until after the war. W.E.B. Du Bois, an influential black leader, agreed. He wrote an editorial in *Crisis* magazine urging black editors to tone down their editorials. "Let us, while this war lasts, forget our special grievances and close ranks shoulder to shoulder with our own fellow citizens."[57]

Most papers followed Du Bois's call to support the war effort. Some, like Abbott's *Defender* and the *Washington Bee*, kept printing militant editorials about black soldiers' treatment. The *Bee*'s editor, William Calvin Chase, wrote:

> But the Negro is willing today to take up arms and defend the American flag. . . . His mother, sister, brother and children are being burned at the stake and yet the American flag is his em-

blem and which he stands ready to defend. In all the battles the Negro soldier has proved his loyalty and today he is the only true American at whom the finger of scorn cannot be pointed.[58]

Race Riots Explode

After the war, blacks hoped that black soldiers' achievements would help them gain respect and improve race relations. "When this war shall have ceased the Negro will have assumed his rightful place in the opinions of Americans. He could then assert himself as a man—not as a black man—as a man,"[59] wrote Robert Vann, *Pittsburgh Courier* editor.

White children cheer outside a black family's home that they set on fire during the "Red Summer" of 1919.

Black veterans came home from the war hoping to be treated like heroes. They quickly grew frustrated when they found white attitudes had not changed. Many refused to back down meekly when faced with discrimination at home. This new defiance angered many whites. They also feared that blacks would use their military training to demand equality. Adding to the tension, many northern cities were swollen and overcrowded as black workers arrived from the south.

Rising tensions finally reached the breaking point. Race riots erupted around the country between 1919 and 1921. In fact, the summer of 1919 became known as the "Red Summer" because of its violence. Hundreds of people died, with some of the most violent riots occurring in Chicago, Washington D.C., and Elaine, Arkansas. Most of the victims of the violence were black Americans. Some were war veterans.

White papers writing about the riots often blamed blacks. They minimized white roles in the violence. To counter, the black press printed their own riot accounts. Some presented a moderate view. Others, like the *Defender*, ran eye-grabbing, sensational headlines. The *Defender* even printed a box score during the riots. It listed statistics of dead and injured in two columns, one for whites and one for blacks. Many felt the *Defender*'s racial box score encouraged additional violence as each side tried to even the score.

Who Was to Blame?

During the riots black papers and editors openly criticized the white community and government. Whites accused these editors of being Communists. Robert Vann responded: "The conclusion therefore is: as long as the Negro submits to lynching, burnings, and oppressions—and says nothing, he is a loyal American citizen. But when he decides that lynching and burnings shall cease even at the cost of some human bloodshed in America, then he is a Bolshevist."[60]

The Justice Department investigated black newspapers for their role in the riots. In a 1919 report the department claimed "that the black press must assume much of the responsibility for the summer riots and that their constant protests against disfranchisement and lynching were incendiary."[61] Apparently in agreement, the *Defender's* Robert Abbott signed a Chicago Commission on Race Relations report that recommended the black press take more care when presenting racial news.

Black Papers in the Community

As blacks moved north new black papers served the growing communities. By the early 1920s nearly five hundred black papers were in print. These papers helped readers live in a segregated world. The papers printed information about shops and jobs without discrimination. They ran stories about local news. In areas with substandard housing, papers ran campaigns to improve housing. Other papers called for equal pay for all teachers, black or white. The sports and society pages featured black athletes and community members.

Black reporters were popular. "Being an entertainer or an athlete was the only thing more glamorous than being a—a member of the black press with your by-line out there so people could see you. And the reporters and, ah, the columnists became stars in their communities. Everyone knew them. . . . When they walked into a club or restaurant, everyone was excited,"[62] said Phyl Garland of the *Pittsburgh Courier*.

Black Papers as Employers

As black papers grew they became major employers for the black community. Black papers trained black newspapermen and newspaperwomen. Large papers needed workers to run printing presses. They also hired drivers for delivery trucks and newsboys and newsgirls to sell and deliver papers.

Black papers also launched several black artists and writers. Author and poet Langston Hughes worked as a correspondent in the 1930s. Future Pulitzer Prize winner Gwendolyn Brooks wrote poetry for the *Chicago Defender*. Artist Romare Bearden drew cartoons for the *Afro-American* in 1936.

The *Pittsburgh Courier*

The Great Depression caused some black newspapers to fail. Others, however, grew stronger. One paper, the *Pittsburgh Courier*, would eventually surpass the *Chicago Defender* as the most widely read black newspaper.

The Murphys and the *Afro-American*

In 1892 ex-slave John H. Murphy Sr. borrowed two hundred dollars from his wife to buy a small black newspaper, the *Afro-American*. At the time the paper advertised church and community events. Murphy, who whitewashed walls and fences for a living, jumped into a publishing career that would last for generations. He expanded the paper to include current issues and events. The *Afro-American* became one of the most widely read black newspapers in the South and East.

Over the years new generations of the Murphy family took their places in the *Afro-American*. During World War II Elizabeth Murphy Phillips became the first black woman to serve as a war correspondent.

Before his death in 1922, Murphy Sr. wrote a credo for his paper:

> A newspaper succeeds because its management believes in itself, in God and in the present generation. It must always ask itself—
>
> Whether it has kept faith with the common people;
>
> Whether it has no other goal except to see that their liberties are preserved and their future assured;
>
> Whether it is fighting to get rid of slums, to provide jobs for everybody;
>
> Whether it stays out of politics except to expose corruption and condemn injustice, race prejudice and the cowardice of compromise.

Quoted in Armistead S. Pride and Clint C. Wilson II, *A History of the Black Press*. Washington, DC: Howard University Press, 1997, p. 135.

On January 15, 1910, the *Pittsburgh Courier's* first issue hit the streets. Pittsburgh attorney Robert Vann was one of the men who organized the paper. When the first editor quit, Vann took the job. The paper started slowly, but Vann saw potential to expand. He hired Ira Lewis as a sportswriter in 1914. Lewis was a talented salesman, and he quickly built up ads and circulation. Lewis eventually would become the paper's business manager and second in command behind Vann.

The *Courier* did not run splashy headlines in red ink like the *Chicago Defender*. Instead it used a peach-colored cover page to attract attention. Vann printed front-page editorials about causes he felt were important. He urged businesses to hire black workers as well as European immigrants. He criticized unions that refused to admit black members. He spotlighted the need for better housing and education. Sometimes Vann called for boycotts of businesses that did not treat blacks fairly.

The *Courier* Expands

Through World War I the *Courier* was similar to many black papers around the country. Vann, however, had bigger dreams. He wanted to earn more money and decided to make several changes. First he printed *Courier* editions in different cities. Editions appeared in New York, St. Louis, and Chicago. The *Courier* became one of the first truly national black newspapers.

Vann also hired talented black journalists. At its peak the *Courier* had fifteen columnists. The radical W.E.B. Du Bois, journalist George Schulyer, who was known for his conservative

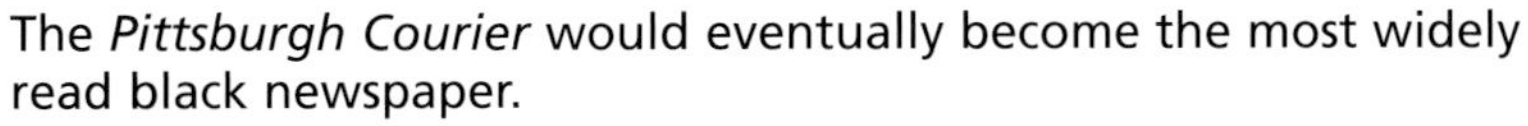

The *Pittsburgh Courier* would eventually become the most widely read black newspaper.

views, and influential leader Marcus Garvey all wrote articles and editorials for the *Courier*. The *Courier* prided itself on featuring diverse opinions. First Vann would run one side of a position. The following week he would run the opposite position. Vann believed debate would increase the paper's circulation. His strategies quickly proved to be correct.

By 1936 the *Courier* reached a circulation of 174,000. It had become an important and influential paper. Many people believed the *Courier* was the best all-around black newspaper of the time. Said Robert Lavelle, a *Courier* employee:

> The Courier represented hope for me. The hope that things could be better for me and the hope that some of the things that I knew needed to be done could be done and I recognized the power of the press at that time. There wasn't television and, ah, there wasn't radio, you know, was certainly present, but we didn't have access to it. But we did have access to newspapers.[63]

Although Robert Vann died in 1940, he had shown how to achieve success without extremes like Abbott's *Defender*. The *Courier* gained fame for tact, diplomacy, accuracy, and finding stories with race appeal.

World War II

On December 7, 1941, Japanese planes bombed Pearl Harbor. The United States entered World War II with a flurry of patriotism. For blacks the dilemma faced in World War I still existed. Why should blacks fight for democracy abroad when their rights at home were denied?

Once again the black press supported the country. They encouraged blacks to enlist in the military. Black papers highlighted black achievements in the war and at home.

Just as during World War I, segregation in the military was still common. Black soldiers often trained and worked in separate units. They had separate mess halls, barracks, and bars. Even the blood supply was segregated. In addition, promotions of black officers were rare. Often black troops served under white commanding officers. In camps where blacks and whites were together, white soldiers often taunted and treated blacks poorly.

Sports at the *Pittsburgh Courier*

The *Pittsburgh Courier* was well known for its top-notch sports coverage. The paper hired sportswriters to focus on black athletes. These writers covered stories like Jesse Owens's Olympic victories. The *Courier's* sports staff also recognized the potential of a young, unknown boxer named Joe Louis. They followed his fights and career as he rose to become one of the greatest heavyweight fighters of all time.

Sportswriter Wendell Smith and the *Courier* campaigned for the integration of Major League Baseball. In the early 1900s black players were not allowed to play for white Major League ball clubs. Instead they played in a separate Negro league. Smith used his *Courier* columns to protest baseball segregation. With Smith's efforts and help, black baseball player Jackie Robinson broke the color barrier in 1947 when he signed with the Major League's Brooklyn Dodgers.

Boxer Joe Louis.

During World War II, black soldiers were often trained and served in separate units.

The black press did not remain silent on the abuses and discrimination in the armed forces. Said Patrick Washburn, a professor at Ohio University's E.W. Scripps School of Journalism: "I mean all of these injustices keep on happening and the black press is playing up all of 'em. And the important thing is, the black press says, 'This time, unlike World War I, we aren't backing down. We are not going to just join the government in this war and stop complaining.' They did it in World War I. They said, 'We aren't doing it this time.'"[64]

Double V Campaign

During World War II the *Courier* thrived under Ira Lewis's leadership. The paper emerged to lead the fight for black civil rights and fair treatment of black soldiers. Lewis printed columns about blacks being excluded from military officer ranks. The *Courier* criticized the navy for using blacks only as chambermaids, bellhops, and dishwashers.

A letter from James Thompson, a Kansas cafeteria worker, inspired the *Courier*'s famous Double V campaign. He wrote:

> Should I sacrifice my life to live half-American? Will things be better for the next generation in the peace to follow? Would it be demanding too much to demand full citizenship rights in exchange for the sacrificing of my life? The V for victory sign is being displayed prominently in all so-called democratic countries which are fighting for victory over aggression, slavery and tyranny. Let we colored Americans adopt the double VV for a double Victory. The first V for victory over our enemies from without, the second V for victory over our enemies from within.[65]

Thousands of letters and telegrams poured into the *Courier*. They supported James Thompson's idea. The *Courier* staff launched its Double V campaign. They designed a Double V diagram with an eagle in the middle. Quickly, the Double V spread like wildfire. Said Washburn:

> You had women walking around with Double Vs on their dresses. You had a new hairstyle called the "doubler" where black women would walk around and weave two

> Vs in their hair. You had Double V baseball games, Double V flag-[waving] ceremonies, Double V gardens. . . . And the *Pittsburgh Courier*, which was looking for circulation, played this to the hilt.[66]

The Military Tries to Suppress Black Papers

During World War II tensions rose in military camps over the inferior treatment of black soldiers. Before long, fights broke out between black and white military men. White papers usually ignored these stories. Black newspapers, however, ran front-page headlines on these military race riots.

Some commanders thought the black press's criticism of the military hurt soldier morale. They tried to stop soldiers from reading black papers. Some banned the papers; others ordered newsboys off the bases. Said Washburn:

> On a number of bases you had papers that were taken away from newsboys, black newspapers taken away from newsboys and they—and they had paper burnings. I mean you think about the fact that you had books that were burned in Germany before World War II and people thought how bad that was. Well, you had newspaper burnings in World War II in this country.[67]

Government Investigation

The federal government blamed black papers and the *Courier's* Double V campaign for low morale in the black community. J. Edgar Hoover, director of the FBI, believed the black press threatened America's war effort. He thought that campaigns like the Double V were the work of traitors during wartime. With his support several government agencies launched investigations of black editors. They sent agents to the newspapers' offices to report on antigovernment activity.

In 1942 Hoover presented a report to Attorney General Francis Biddle on the black press's activities. He asked Biddle to indict several publishers for treason. John Sengstacke, nephew of Robert Abbott and publisher of the *Chicago Defender*, was alarmed at the serious charges. He traveled to Washington in June 1942 to speak with Biddle.

At the meeting Biddle spread several black papers on a table. Biddle told Sengstacke that the papers were hurting the war effort. He threatened to take the black publishers to court under the Espionage Act. In an interview Sengstacke remembered his reply. "I said, 'What are we supposed to do about it? These are facts and we aren't gonna stop. That's what it's all about.' That's what the black press was all about, protecting blacks in this country."[68]

Sengstacke explained the black press's position, and the two men came to an agreement. If the press would not increase their criticisms during the rest of the war, Biddle would not prosecute them. Sengstacke said, "After we explained to them what the problem was and we were citizens like everybody else and wanted to be, they had no problem with it."[69]

Time to Turn Lincoln's Picture to the Wall

In addition to his work at the *Pittsburgh Courier*, Robert Vann was also interested in politics. Like many blacks he was originally a member of the Republican Party. The Republicans were Abraham Lincoln's party, the party that had given blacks their freedom. Vann, however, grew increasingly dissatisfied with the Republican Party. He felt that the Republicans were taking black voters for granted and not doing enough to help the community. In 1932 Vann switched to the Democratic Party and supported Franklin D. Roosevelt's presidential campaign. In a speech in Cleveland, Vann said: "It is a mistaken idea that the Negro must wait until the party selects him. . . . I see million[s] of Negroes turning the picture of Lincoln to the wall. This year I see Negroes voting a Democratic ticket." These words inspired many blacks to vote Democratic and help elect Roosevelt. After the election Vann was rewarded for bringing black voters to the Democratic Party. The new administration appointed him as an assistant attorney general.

Quoted in Andrew Buni, *Robert L. Vann of the Pittsburgh Courier: Politics and Black Journalism*. Pittsburgh, PA: University of Pittsburgh Press, 1974, p. 194.

Publisher John Sengstacke defended the right of the black press to criticize the segregation of black soldiers.

Other government offices supported the black papers against antigovernment and Communist charges. The Office of War Information issued a report that "the Negro press has never advocated the overthrow of the present form of government and has never upheld a philosophy or a policy alien to constitutional formulations of the American way of life."[70]

The Campaign at Home Continues

By the end of the war, the black press had reached all-time highs in popularity and circulation. More than 2 million papers circulated each week. It had survived despite several government attempts to suppress its message. The black press had reached its pinnacle of power and influence.

Vernon Jarrett, a *Chicago Defender* journalist, remembered the postwar feeling. "The Double V campaign said, 'When you come back home, we want the world to be different.' It was that simple. And it inspired . . . I came back home with that feeling, that I'm not gonna take what I used to take, that I'm not going to let them insult my mother and father the way they once did because we are going to fight back."[71]

The 1950s and 1960s would provide the black press with new challenges. The civil rights movement would achieve many of the black press's goals. Unfortunately, those successes would ultimately close the door on the black press's greatest era.

Chapter Six

The Civil Rights Era and Beyond

For more than a century, black editors served a neglected community. They hoped their words would convince America that blacks deserved the same rights and treatment as whites. They also realized that achieving this dream would eventually put many black papers out of business. If white society and papers treated blacks as equals, there would no longer be a need for the black paper.

The Civil Rights Movement Begins

In the 1950s the black community became more vocal about the need for change. Once again the black press led the campaign for civil rights. Black papers and communities called for equal voting rights. They wanted access to the same public places as whites. Blacks wanted their children to have the same school education as whites. They also wanted the same job and housing opportunities as whites.

On May 17, 1954, the Supreme Court issued a landmark decision in *Brown v. Board of Education of Topeka, Kansas*. In the decision, the Court banned segregation of schools by race. This decision sent shock waves across the country and angered southern whites. Tensions came to a head in Little Rock, Arkansas. When officials tried

An Arkansas National Guard member escorts nine black students leaving Little Rock's Central High School. The Guard was called in after violence erupted when the school was integrated.

The National Newspaper Publishers Association

In 1940 John Sengstacke, nephew of Robert Abbott and publisher of the *Chicago Defender*, invited the leading black publishers for a meeting in Chicago. He wanted to bring together the men and women of the black press to harmonize "our energies in a common purpose for the benefit of Negro journalism." Other black professional groups, like physicians, lawyers, and clergy, had benefited from national organizations. Sengstacke believed it was time publishers did the same. The first step was coming together and meeting each other. They could talk about advertising and editorial and newsgathering issues. They could share advice and learn from each other.

Representatives from twenty-two publications traveled to Chicago. They decided to form the National Negro Publishers Association. In 1956 the group changed their name to the National Newspaper Publishers Association (NNPA).

Today more than two hundred black newspapers are members of the NNPA. Their publications reach over 15 million readers. The NNPA has created an electronic news service and a Web site, Black Press USA, which allow the black press to provide up-to-the minute news to readers.

to integrate the school, they met resistance from white mobs and government officials. Images of the violence in Little Rock swept through newspapers and television. Eventually, President Eisenhower sent the Arkansas National Guard to Little Rock to take control and regain calm. Although Little Rock had calmed, the civil rights movement was just beginning.

Montgomery Bus Boycott

Another significant event occurred the next year in Montgomery, Alabama. In 1955 a young black woman named Rosa Parks was arrested when she refused to give up her bus seat to a white man. Black leaders, including a young Martin Luther King Jr., organized a bus boycott to protest Parks's arrest and bus segregation. The Montgomery bus boycott stretched for months and impacted many Montgomery businesses.

Montgomery officials tried to stop the boycott by arresting protesters. Sometimes violence erupted. Evelyn Cunningham, a reporter for the *Pittsburgh Courier*, traveled to Montgomery to cover the story. Cunningham said:

> Hell was breaking loose Down South. This young man, this young preacher in Montgomery was beginning to appear in the papers and I wanted to get down there. . . . I am in one of those sad little hotels in Montgomery . . . when I heard a bomb. . . . The man at the desk told me . . . they had bombed Dr. King's house. Ah, so I dashed over to Dr. King's house and, sure enough, the front of the house was demolished. . . . You have no idea the impact of standing there watching this young man plead with these hundreds of people who were standing in front of his house with Coke bottles and pipes getting ready to go into town and beat up somebody, to watch him tell them to be calm, to be calm, that was not the way. So I wasn't about to leave the South with my introduction to Dr. King that way at that point.[72]

Sit-Ins and Protests

In the late 1950s and early 1960s, black youth grew impatient. They were tired of waiting for the government to act on civil rights issues. They decided to take matters into their own hands. They organized sit-ins and protests to push for integration of public places like lunch counters, beaches, and libraries. At first the demonstrations were peaceful. As they spread throughout the South, protesters faced insults, bomb threats, and physical violence.

Many northern black newspapers carried stories about the events in the South. The *Pittsburgh Courier* even published a list of tips to help students fighting segregation. The list included items like "Don't strike back or curse back if abused," and "Show yourself friendly and courteous at all times."[73]

Competition from White Journalists

For decades the white press had ignored the black community. Now they realized that the civil rights movement was one of the century's biggest stories. White papers sent reporters to cover events as they happened. Television stations also sent reporters to

African Americans pushed for equality by organizing protests and sit-ins at lunch counters, like this one, and other public places.

film footage as it happened. For the first time blacks had a choice about where to learn about their community, interests, and leaders.

Unfortunately, many black newspapers could not compete with the daily white press and television. By the time they printed their weekly issue, it was filled with old news. Few black newspapers had the money or staff to send reporters around the country for firsthand reports. Instead, black journalists often covered events via phone or rewrote news accounts published in white papers.

Ironically, few southern black newspapers covered the civil rights events happening in their own backyard. Said Cunningham:

> The black press in the South really did not give as much to those struggles in those days as they might have. I don't think they sent their best reporters. . . . And at that point I think they were very, very embarrassed that these ugly things were happening on their turf . . . which is one way I think of pretending that it wasn't as bad as it was, in some instances to the extreme that it doesn't exist, these problems.[74]

Changing Roles

As the civil rights movement took hold, the black press's role slowly changed. For years the black press had been the black community's champion. Its publishers and editors led protests against injustice and calls for equality. Now the black community was no longer content to let the black press fight their battles. They took the call for change into their own hands.

The black press slowly became less of a fighter. Often black newspapers simply reported on events and news made by other people. Still, papers like the *Chicago Defender* continued to print sharp editorials. On May 16, 1961, the *Defender* ran pictures of a white mob attacking a Freedom Riders' bus in Alabama. The Freedom Riders were black and white volunteers who traveled to Alabama and Mississippi to challenge segregation in the transit system. In its editorial the *Defender* criticized law enforcement's handling of the violence:

> What is still more revolting is the posture of indifference of the local authorities under whose very eyes the disgraceful drama was enacted. Here you have police officers sworn to

uphold the law, to keep peace and order, yet they chose the role of disinterested, impassive spectators while peaceful men were being assaulted and slammed almost to death.[75]

Integration of the Press

At first white papers used white staff reporters for stories on the civil rights movement. Black journalists at white papers or on television were rare. That changed when several black communities went up in flames during the late 1960s.

Members of the Freedom Riders watch as the bus they were on burns after a white mob slashed the tires and set the bus on fire on May 14, 1961.

A series of riots spread across the country from Watts in Los Angeles to Harlem in New York. White editors realized that they needed staff that could go into black communities and get the inside story from residents. For the first time the white papers turned to black journalists. Said Phyl Garland:

> White newspapers and television wanted to find what was going on, so they hired black reporters in any numbers for the first time. And I know friends of mine who moved into mainstream at that time. They could cite the particular riot that led to their being hired. I remember sitting in the *Courier* news room and watching people disappear. They were going on to other jobs.[76]

Job offers from white papers easily tempted black journalists. White papers paid more money, often printed daily issues, and had larger, more national audiences. "The reason why I didn't stay

The Kerner Report

In 1967 President Lyndon Johnson formed the Kerner commission to explain the causes of recent race riots. In their 1968 report the commission had harsh words for the white press:

> The news media have failed to analyze and report adequately on racial problems in the United States and, as a related matter, to meet the Negro's legitimate expectations in journalism. By and large, news organizations have failed to communicate to both their black and white audiences a sense of the problems America faces and the sources of potential solutions. The media report and write from the standpoint of a white man's world. The ills of the ghetto, the difficulties of life there, the Negro's burning sense of grievance, are seldom conveyed. Slights and indignities are part of the Negro's daily life, and many of them come from what he now calls "the white press"—a press that repeatedly, if unconsciously, reflects the biases, the paternalism, the indifference of white America. This may be understandable, but it is not excusable in an institution that has the mission to inform and educate the whole of our society.

The report resulted in the white press hiring more black journalists and developing journalist training programs.

Quoted in History Matters, "'The Communications Media, Ironically, Have Failed to Communicate': The Kerner Report Assesses Media Coverage of Riots and Race Relations." http://historymatters.gmu.edu/d/6553.

with the black newspaper, the black press, and I loved it—it was a freedom that a reporter dreamed of—is because of the money, the financial situation. I had a family I had to support and as a result, I was offered more money from Westinghouse Broadcasting,"[77] said George Barbour, a reporter with the *Pittsburgh Courier*.

Generation Gap

As the black press faced challenges from white papers and television, it also had internal challenges. Black editors had always been leaders in the community. They had been at the forefront of the civil rights fight. Their papers targeted the black middle class. They partnered with established organizations like the National Association for the Advancement of Colored People and the National Urban League. These organizations were founded in the early 1900s and had become premier civil rights champions for the black community.

The rising black youth of the 1960s had their own ideas. Many were poor and lived in city ghettos. They dismissed the traditional black press as too conservative and irrelevant. Instead they created underground tabloid publications that filled ghettos. Civil rights organizations also printed their own publications. Both competed with the traditional black press and caused its circulation to drop.

The Decline of the Black Press

The changes of the 1960s and 1970s devastated the black press. Television and white papers provided more immediate news. Youth papers and civil rights publications drew readers away from traditional black papers. As readers turned to competitors, circulation dropped. As white papers hired black journalists, the black press struggled without their brightest talent. The quality of their papers declined.

The civil rights legislation in the 1960s achieved many goals of the black press. Some believed this success caused the black press to lose direction. In 1977 Enoc Waters, a retired *Chicago Defender* editor, said: "The disturbing question . . . is that the black press lost its sense of mission in the last decade. In my days, the total commitment was to advancing the cause that called for the birth of the Negro press. We were not only black newsmen but we

The black press partnered with organizations like the NAACP to support the civil rights movement.

regarded ourselves as a specialized division of a vast black civil rights crusade."[78]

In addition, successful black editors from the 1940s and 1950s, like C.B. Powell of the New York *Amsterdam News* and Leon Washington of the Los Angeles *Sentinel*, were aging. Many had retired or died by the 1970s. Unfortunately for their papers, replacements did not have the same prestige and vision. Many were hesitant to try new ideas. The sharp editorials that had drawn so many readers to these papers disappeared. Readers turned away.

By 1977 the *Chicago Defender's* daily circulation sank to thirty-four thousand. The *Pittsburgh Courier* reported a weekly circulation of only thirty thousand. As circulation declined, advertisers pulled ads. With readers and ads dropping, many black newspapers faced bankruptcy and disappeared.

Many regretted the loss of powerful black papers. "The black press today seems to react only, react to a—an issue or a situation or react to something that's in the white press. We very rarely in our black press today initiate, dig up stories of our own. . . . I think we do need a black press today, very, very much so,"[79] said Cunningham.

New Challenges for Black Journalists

Black journalists also faced new challenges. As they took jobs with the white press, they lost the black paper's close-knit family. Now they were isolated in newsrooms across the country. They still faced discrimination. Although they reported the news, few black journalists achieved management or decision-making roles. In addition, many journalists complained that black promotions were slower than their white coworkers'.

Black journalists working for white papers also had to decide what was more important to them—their race or their job. Many white papers still followed policies that portrayed the black community negatively. They reported stories where blacks were criminals, drug addicts, and welfare mothers. These papers rarely ran stories about a hardworking, middle-class black family.

If a black journalist wrote a negative story about the black community, friends and neighbors criticized him or her. But if the journalist did not report the story, he or she could get in trouble

Black Magazines

Black magazines thrived after the civil rights movement. Many were not originally designed as protest vehicles. That left them better able than the black newspapers to change with the times. John H. Johnson was one of the greatest black magazine publishers. He built his empire in 1942 with his first magazine, *Negro Digest*. It was a monthly magazine and featured stories about black accomplishments and news items for the black community. The *Negro Digest* also ran articles by prominent whites on black issues.

Johnson launched his second magazine, *Ebony*, in 1945. It was similar to the popular *Life* magazine and featured lots of glossy pictures. By 1967 *Ebony* became the first black monthly to reach circulation of 1 million. It would eventually become one of the all-time black magazine leaders.

Johnson's success in building his magazine empire happened in part because he excelled at changing with the times. He introduced and closed magazines as public tastes changed. He also worked hard to attract large white advertisers to his magazines.

By the 1970s many in the black community made economic and educational gains. Magazines like *Essence* and *Black Enterprise* emerged as major publications. They targeted the newly affluent black consumer.

with the editor. This dilemma was highlighted in 1984 when the Reverend Jesse Jackson ran for the Democratic presidential nomination. A black journalist for the *Washington Post* reported that Jackson had called Jews "hymies." Support for Jackson's presidential campaign declined. Some criticized the reporter for not considering the effect his story would have on the black community.

The Future of the Black Press

The black press had risen out of the needs of the black community. Over the years it served as a champion and teacher. It unified, inspired, and gave hope to millions of black Americans. "The black press was the advocate of all our dreams, wishes and desires. I still think it was a greatest advocate for equal and civil rights that black people ever had in America. It had an effect on everybody,"[80] said reporter Frank Bolden.

The civil rights movement meant the black press had achieved many goals originally sought by pioneers Samuel Cornish and John Russwurm. Many people believed this success would end the black press. Thomas W. Young, president of the Negro Newspaper Publishing Association, predicted, "The more closely it approaches success, the nearer it propels itself to the brink of oblivion. And if it should eventually succeed in helping to create the kind of society for which it strives, the Negro Press will have contrived its own extinction."[81] As black papers declined in the 1970s, it appeared his words might be coming true.

Others disagree. Although newspapers, television, and radio are now integrated, many blacks believe the media does not adequately

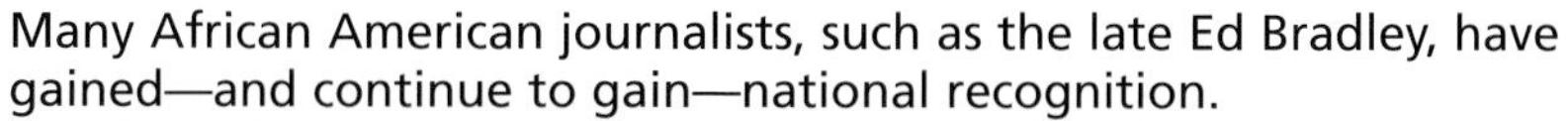

Many African American journalists, such as the late Ed Bradley, have gained—and continue to gain—national recognition.

represent the black community. In a 2001 study titled "Off Balance: Youth, Race and Crime in the News," researchers found that racial bias in the media still exists. According to the study:

> A disproportionate number of perpetrators on the news are people of color, especially African Americans, and the strongest evidence shows that people of color, again primarily African Americans, are under-represented as victims in crime news. African American perpetrators are depicted as dangerous and indistinguishable as a group, and they appear more frequently in crime news stories than Whites.[82]

Until media bias disappears, many believe there will be a need for the black press.

Even though the black press's power and influence has diminished, it still thrives in many cities today. Papers like the *Winston-Salem Chronicle*, the *Miami Times*, and the *St. Louis American* continue the legacy of the black press. Black journalists like Carl T. Rowan, the late Ed Bradley of CBS, and Dorothy Gilliam of the *Washington Post* have gained national recognition.

Despite challenges many believe the black press will exist as long as there is a black community in America. Robert W. Bogle is the editor of the *Philadelphia Tribune*, currently the oldest surviving black newspaper. On the future of the black press, Bogle wrote:

> To paraphrase Mark Twain, rumors of our demise have been greatly exaggerated. The black press is very much alive and well. Though we are struggling with issues facing all newspapers, our reason for being remains strong. And we have not [wavered] in our commitment to our readers. We plan to continue to serve the African American communities around the nation with the information that helps them survive and prosper in a dynamic society.[83]

Notes

Introduction: A Voice for the Black Community

1. Samuel Cornish and John Russwurm, *Freedom's Journal*, March 16, 1827, p. 1. www.wisconsinhistory.org/library archives/aanp/freedom/docs/v1n01 .pdf.
2. Quoted in PBS, *The Black Press: Soldiers Without Swords*. www.pbs.org/blackpress/film/index .html.
3. Quoted in Armistead S. Pride and Clint C. Wilson II, *A History of the Black Press*. Washington, DC: Howard University Press, 1997, p. xi.

Chapter One: The Birth of the Black Press

4. Quoted in Pride and Wilson, *A History of the Black Press*, p. 7.
5. Quoted in US History.org, "The Declaration of Independence." www.ushistory.org/Declaration/ document/index.htm.
6. Quoted in Charles A. Simmons, *The African American Press: With Special Reference to Four Newspapers, 1827–1965*. Jefferson, NC: McFarland, 1998, pp. 9–10.
7. Cornish and Russwurm, *Freedom's Journal*, p. 1.
8. Cornish and Russwurm, *Freedom's Journal*, p. 1.
9. Cornish and Russwurm, *Freedom's Journal*, p. 1.
10. Cornish and Russwurm, *Freedom's Journal*, p. 1.
11. John Russwurm, *Freedom's Journal*, March 14, 1829, p. 3. http://www.wisconsinhistory.org/ libraryarchives/aanp/freedom/ docs/v2n50.pdf.
12. Russwurm, *Freedom's Journal*, p. 3.
13. Quoted in Pride and Wilson, *A History of the Black Press*, p. 23.

Chapter Two: Antebellum Papers and the Civil War

14. Quoted in Discovering U.S. History, "Text of the Pro-Slavery Argument, 1832," Gale Research, 1997.
15. William Lloyd Garrison, "On the Constitution and the Union," Teaching American History. http://teachingamericanhistory .org/library/index.asp?document =570.
16. *Colored American*, "Title of This Journal," National Humanities Center. http://nationalhumanities center.org/pds/maai/community/ text6/coloredamerican.pdf.
17. *Colored American*, "Serious Reflections," National Humanities

Center. http://nationalhumanitiescenter.org/pds/maai/community/text6/coloredamerican.pdf.
18. Quoted in Pride and Wilson, *A History of the Black Press*, pp. 47–48.
19. Willis Hodges, *Free Man of Color*, WorkLore. www.worklore.net/images/acrobat/RacialBias-WillisHodges.pdf.
20. Hodges, *Free Man of Color*.
21. Hodges, *Free Man of Color*.
22. Hodges, *Free Man of Color*.
23. Quoted in Roland E. Wolseley, *The Black Press, U.S.A.* Ames: Iowa State University Press, 1971, p. 23.
24. *North Star*, December 3, 1847, p. 1. Maryland State Archives. www.msa.md.gov/msa/speccol/sc5600/sc5604/2004/december/images/front_page_18471203.pdf.
25. John C. Calhoun, "The Clay Compromise Measures," National Center for Public Policy Research. www.nationalcenter.org/CalhounClayCompromise.html.

Chapter Three: The Black Press and Reconstruction

26. Quoted in Martin E. Dann, *The Black Press (1827–1890): The Quest for National Identity*. New York: G.P. Putnam's Sons, 1971, p. 338.
27. Quoted in Frederick G. Detweiler, *The Negro Press in the United States*. College Park, MD: McGrath, 1968, p. 51.
28. Quoted in Dann, *The Black Press*, p. 339.
29. Quoted in Dann, *The Black Press*, p. 359.
30. Quoted in U.S. Constitution Online, "U.S. Constitution—Amendment 14." www.usconstitution.net/xconst_Am14.html.
31. Quoted in Dann, *The Black Press*, p. 102.
32. Quoted in Simmons, *The African American Press*, p. 17.
33. Quoted in Lee A. Baker, "Ida B. Wells-Barnett and Her Passion for Justice," Duke University, April 1996. www.duke.edu/~ldbaker/classes/AAIH/caaih/ibwells/ibwbkgrd.html.
34. Quoted in PBS, *The Black Press*.
35. Quoted in Simmons, *The African American Press*, p. 19.
36. Quoted in Simmons, *The African American Press*, p. 19.
37. Ida B. Wells, *Crusade for Justice: The Autobiography of Ida B. Wells*. Chicago: University of Chicago Press, 1970, pp. 62–63.
38. Quoted in Dann, *The Black Press*, p. 106.
39. Quoted in Dann, *The Black Press*, p. 113.
40. Quoted in Wolseley, *The Black Press, U.S.A.*, p. 33.

Chapter Four: The Increasing Power of the Press

41. Quoted in Dann, *The Black Press*, p. 349.
42. Quoted in Dann, *The Black Press*, p. 114.

43. Quoted in *The Rise and Fall of Jim Crow*, "Civil Rights Act of 1875 Declared Unconstitutional," PBS. www.pbs.org/wnet/jimcrow/stories_events_uncivil.html.
44. Quoted in Pride and Wilson, *A History of the Black Press*, p. 122.
45. Quoted in Simmons, *The African American Press*, p. 22.
46. Quoted in Pride and Wilson, *A History of the Black Press*, p. 123.
47. Quoted in Pride and Wilson, *A History of the Black Press*, p. 124.
48. Quoted in Simmons, *The African American Press*, p. 23.
49. Quoted in PBS, *The Black Press*.
50. Quoted in PBS, *The Black Press*.
51. Quoted in PBS, *The Black Press*.
52. Quoted in PBS, *The Black Press*.

Chapter Five: Wartime and Depression

53. Quoted in Simmons, *The African American Press*, p. 33.
54. Quoted in PBS, *The Black Press*.
55. Quoted in PBS, *The Black Press*.
56. Quoted in Simmons, *The African American Press*, p. 33.
57. Quoted in Simmons, *The African American Press*, p. 39.
58. Quoted in Wolseley, *The Black Press, U.S.A.*, p. 53.
59. Quoted in Simmons, *The African American Press*, p. 46.
60. Quoted in Simmons, *The African American Press*, p. 47.
61. Quoted in Simmons, *The African American Press*, p. 47.
62. Quoted in PBS, *The Black Press*.
63. Quoted in PBS, *The Black Press*.
64. Quoted in PBS, *The Black Press*.
65. Quoted in Simmons, *The African American Press*, p. 80.
66. Quoted in PBS, *The Black Press*.
67. Quoted in PBS, *The Black Press*.
68. Quoted in PBS, *The Black Press*.
69. Quoted in PBS, *The Black Press*.
70. Quoted in Simmons, *The African American Press*, p. 87.
71. Quoted in PBS, *The Black Press*.

Chapter Six: The Civil Rights Era and Beyond

72. Quoted in PBS, *The Black Press*.
73. Quoted in Simmons, *The African American Press*, p. 98.
74. Quoted in PBS, *The Black Press*.
75. Quoted in Simmons, *The African American Press*, p. 113.
76. Quoted in PBS, *The Black Press*.
77. Quoted in PBS, *The Black Press*.
78. Quoted in Pride and Wilson, *A History of the Black Press*, p. 234.
79. Quoted in PBS, *The Black Press*.
80. Quoted in PBS, *The Black Press*.
81. Quoted in Pride and Wilson, *A History of the Black Press*, p. 261.
82. Lori Dorfman and Vincent Schiraldi, "Off Balance: Youth, Race and Crime in the News," Building Blocks for Youth. www.buildingblocksforyouth.org/media/exec.html.
83. Quoted in Pride and Wilson, *A History of the Black Press*, p. 268.

Time Line

1827

Samuel Cornish and John Russwurm publish the first issue of *Freedom's Journal*.

1829

Freedom's Journal ceases publication. David Walker publishes his antislavery pamphlet *Walker's Appeal*.

1847

Frederick Douglass publishes the first issue of the *North Star*.

1862

The first black newspaper in the South, *L'Union*, appears.

1864

New Orleans Tribune, the first black daily newspaper, is published in French and English.

1884

T. Thomas Fortune becomes the publisher of the *New York Freeman* (later called the *New York Age*).

1892

Ida B. Wells writes an article denouncing the lynching of three local blacks in Memphis. A white mob vandalizes her printing office and forces her paper, the *Memphis Free Speech*, to shut down.

1901

William Monroe Trotter founds the *Boston Guardian* and strongly opposes Booker T. Washington's policy of accommodation.

1905

Robert Abbott launches the *Chicago Defender*.

1910

Robert Vann takes over as editor of the *Pittsburgh Courier*.

1916

The great migration of blacks to northern cities peaks after encouragement by Robert Abbott and the *Chicago Defender*.

1940

Upon the death of Robert Abbott, his nephew, John Sengstacke, takes over the *Chicago Defender*. Robert Vann dies.

1942

The *Pittsburgh Courier* launches the Double V campaign. The FBI investigates the black press for anti-American activity during wartime.

1955

As the civil rights movement takes hold, white papers begin coverage of national civil rights stories. Black papers struggle to cover rapid daily events across the country.

1964–1965

The Civil Rights Act is passed. It bans discrimination on the basis of race, color, national origin, religion, and sex. White papers begin hiring black journalists.

1975

National Association of Black Journalists founded in Washington, D.C.

For More Information

Books

Chrisanne Beckner, *100 African Americans Who Shaped American History.* New York: Bluewood Books, 1995. Several individuals profiled in this book were editors and writers for black newspapers.

Walter Dean Myers, *Ida B. Wells: Let the Truth Be Told.* New York: Amistad and Collins, 2008. A picture-book biography that traces Wells's life from her birth in slavery to her work for black newspapers.

Armistead S. Pride and Clint C. Wilson II, *A History of the Black Press.* Washington DC: Howard University Press, 1997. A comprehensive review of the history of the black press with descriptions of many papers and key figures.

Carl Senna, *The Black Press and the Struggle for Civil Rights.* New York: Franklin Watts, 1994. A young adult title that traces the history of the black press and emphasizes its role in the civil rights struggle.

Web Sites

BlackNews.com (www.blacknews.com/directory/black_african_american_newspapers.shtml). This Web site has a current listing of daily and weekly black newspapers and links to their Web sites.

***The Black Press: Soldiers Without Swords*, PBS** (www.pbs.org/blackpress/film). This Web site offers a full transcript of the film along with short biographies and interviews with black journalists and historians.

Black Press USA (www.blackpressusa.com). This official Web site of the black press features up-to-the-minute news for the black community and also articles and time lines about the history of the black press.

The History of Jim Crow (www.jimcrowhistory.org/resources/lessonplans/hs_es_black_press.htm). This Web site offers an overview essay of the black press as well as detail about historical events in the struggle for black freedom and rights.

Voices of Civil Rights (www.voicesofcivilrights.org/index.html). This Web site provides information about the civil rights struggle and milestones and also features personal accounts.

Wisconsin Historical Society: African American Newspapers and Periodicals (www.wisconsinhistory.org/libraryarchives/aanp/freedom/). This Web site provides access to digitized online copies of *Freedom's Journal*.

Index

Picture Credits

Cover, Gordon Coster/Time & Life Pictures/Getty Images
© North Wind Picture Archives/Alamy, 29
AP Images, 11, 16, 32, 43, 53, 90
© Bettmann/Corbis, 40, 51, 73, 79, 84, 87, 92–93
© Corbis, 18, 38, 96
© Jack Moebes/Corbis, 44
Courtesy of the FDR Library, 68–69
Gordon Coster/Time & Life Pictures/Getty Images, 61
Herbert Gehr/Time & Life Pictures/Getty Images, 71
The Granger Collection, New York, 22, 30, 59
CBS/Landov, 99
The Library of Congress, 15, 25, 33, 56–57, 64, 77
Schomberg Center for Research in Black Culture, 47

About the Author

Carla Mooney is the author of several books and articles for young readers. A graduate of the University of Pennsylvania, she lives in Pittsburgh, Pennsylvania, with her husband and three children. You can visit her online at www.carla mooney.com.

CHAPEL HILL PUBLIC LIBRARY
TOWN OF CHAPEL HILL
chapelhillpubliclibrary.org